REINVENTING PAUL

REINVENTING PAUL

John G. Gager

OXFORD
UNIVERSITY PRESS

OXFORD

UNIVERSITY PRESS

Oxford   New York
Auckland   Bangkok   Buenos Aires
Cape Town   Chennai   Dar es Salaam   Delhi
Hong Kong   Istanbul   Karachi   Kolkata   Kuala Lumpur   Madrid
Melbourne   Mexico City   Mumbai   Nairobi   São Paulo
Shanghai   Singapore   Taipei   Tokyo   Toronto

and an associated company in

Berlin

Copyright © 2000 by John G. Gager

First published by Oxford University Press, Inc., 2000
198 Madison Avenue, New York, New York 10016

First issued as an Oxford University Press paperback, 2002
Oxford is a registered trademark of Oxford University Press

All rights reserved. No part of this publication may be reproduced,
stored in a retrieval system, or transmitted, in any form or by any
means, electronic, mechanical, photocopying, recording, or otherwise, without the prior permission of Oxford University Press.

Library of Congress Cataloging-in-Publication Data
Gager, John G.
Reinventing Paul / John G. Gager.
p.   cm.
Includes bibliographical references and index.
ISBN 0-19-513474-5 (cloth)   ISBN 0-19-515085-6 (pbk.)
1. Paul, the Apostle, Saint—Views on Judaism.
2. Bible. N.T. Epistles of Paul—Criticism, interpretation, etc.
3. Christianity and other religions—Judaism.
4. Judaism—Relations—Christianity. I. Title.

BS2655.J4 G34 2000   225.9'2—dc21   99-045706

1 3 5 7 9 8 6 4 2
Printed in the United States of America

CONTENTS

PREFACE

lbert Schweitzer once wrote that no task so fully reveals an epoch's understanding of itself as its efforts to write a life of Jesus. But if, as is widely believed, Paul is the second founder of Christianity (Jesus being the first, and the real founder at that) efforts to write about Paul must be even more revealing. I believe that this traditional view of Paul—and Jesus—is wrong. Jesus was not the first founder of Christianity and Paul was not the second. Be that as it may, it still holds true that books on Paul tell us a great deal about the times in which they were written. Now the question arises: Is it possible to break free from this law, from the powerful tendency to read our views into Paul rather than working our way from them? Can we arrive at the "real" Paul? Or, more modestly, at a Paul closer to his time than to ours?

These are not popular questions today. Among many intellectuals, the view is that there is no such thing as the real Paul or any other figure. Only different, shifting, unstable perceptions.

But this does not mean that there are not bad interpretations, even wrong ones. My argument is that the dominant view of Paul across nearly two thousand years is both bad, in that it has proved harmful, and wrong, in that it can no longer be defended historically.

I will use certain terms that require a brief explanation. First, I will rigorously avoid the term *Christianity* when speaking of Jesus, his early followers and Paul. Instead I will employ the term *Jesus-movement*. To some, this may seem like special pleading in that much of my case depends on the claim that the old, bad view of Paul derives from the mistaken assumption that he was Christian. Behind this shift of terms, from Christian to Jesus-movement, lies a much broader contention, namely, that there was no Christianity at all until well after the time of Jesus, his earliest followers, and Paul. In the case of Jesus and his early followers, this position is now taken for granted—they belong totally within the context of first-century Judaism in Roman Palestine and not to the history of later Christianity. To use the term Christian is anachronistic and misleading. The argument here is simple and convincing: the fact that his followers proclaimed Jesus the Messiah (Christ is simply the Greek word used by Jews for the Hebrew *Mashiach*/Messiah) does not place them outside the pale of Judaism. They become Christians only when they begin to view themselves, and are viewed by others, as standing outside, above, or even against Judaism. In other words, this is not a book about early Christianity. In fact, it is not about Christianity at all.

Along with others, I hold that this position must be extended to Paul—and beyond. He, too, belongs to the history of first-century Judaism. Although I will not argue here for an even wider expansion of this position, I believe that it should be applied to other writings in the New Testament, including the Revelation of John, the letter of James, and, among the gospels, Mark and John.

Another term that demands a brief word of explanation is *the law*. I use this word for the Hebrew *Torah*, regularly translated into Greek as *nomos*, into Latin as *lex* and thus into English as law. Although Torah does include a range of properly legal matters (normative rules and regulations of many sorts), it also covers broader notions such as revelation, teaching, and wisdom. It is with respect to these broader notions that the English word law proves inadequate. But it has also been difficult for me and others to come up with a better term. Thus, when I speak of the law or the law of Moses I intend it to be taken in the broadest possible manner. It means everything in and associated with the Pentateuch, the five books attributed to Moses (Genesis, Exodus, Leviticus, Numbers, Deuteronomy). Here I should also note that the designation LXX refers to the Septuagint, the Greek translation of the Hebrew Bible used by Paul and all Greek-speaking Jews of his time.

Preparing and writing this book have generated two unexpected surprises. The first is the legacy of my teachers—Paul Meyer, Nils Dahl, Krister Stendahl, and Ernst Käsemann. In ways that I had not anticipated—though perhaps I should have—I have found myself continually inspired by their work, if not always in predictable ways. I should like to record my gratitude toward them, even while exonerating them from any responsibility for the errors of my ways. The second surprise—though once again perhaps I should have discovered it earlier—was the body of Jewish readers and interpreters of Paul. At least since the mid-eighteenth century, Jewish readers have been both fascinated and puzzled by Paul. By and large, Jewish readers have adopted the old image: Paul holds that God has rejected Judaism and the law; that salvation for Jews lies exclusively through faith in Jesus Christ. At the same time, a curious tension emerges among most Jewish readers. On the one hand, they are far more sensitive than Christians to the Jewish elements in Paul's thinking. For a number of them, Paul emerges as a thoroughly Jewish thinker. On the other hand, many of these same readers have accepted the traditional argument that Paul's negative statements about the law are directed at Jews and, despite his protestations to the contrary, that his rejection of Israel is final. One frequently hears comments like the following: "How could a Jew like Paul say such negative things about the law?"

Two recent dissertations have traced the Jewish dialogue with Paul from the late eighteenth century to the present. In 1990 Nancy Fuchs-Kreimer published *The "Essential Heresy": Paul's View of the Law According to Jewish Writers, 1886–1986* (Ann Arbor, 1990). And in 1996, Stefan Meissner published his *Die Heimholung des Ketzers. Studien zur jüdischen Auseinandersetzung mit Paulus* [The Repatriation/Recovery of the Heretic. Studies on the Jewish Dialogue with Paul](Tübingen, 1996). Both studies emphasize the dramatic shift in views of Paul among a range of recent Jewish writers (Pinchas Lapide, Michael Wyschogrod, Daniel Boyarin, and David Flusser, among others). Like their predecessors, these recent writers stress the Jewish roots and structure of Paul's thoughts. But some of these readers have moved beyond this and have begun to argue that Paul never left Judaism, never repudiated Judaism or its law, and never imagined Israel's redemption in terms of Jesus Christ. They hold that Paul's undeniably negative comments about the law were never directed at the role of the law for Jews but only for the law in relation to Gentiles. They have contributed to a fundamental shift in the way we read and understand the apostle to the Gentiles. At the same time, they have transcended the traditional Jewish assessment of the early Jesus-movement—Jesus, yes; Paul, no—by rediscovering and reclaiming Paul the Jew. No one who ignores these Jewish readers can be taken seriously.

Finally, I must give thanks to those friends who have given helpful comments and encouragement: Martha Himmelfarb, Stanley Stowers, Leigh Gibson, Lloyd Gaston, Cynthia Read, David Satran, Jeffrey Stout, Kristin Gager, and many others.

I dedicate this book to my children—Kristin, Peter, and Andrea. Without them, none of this would have been possible.

Princeton, New Jersey   J.G.
November 1999

REINVENTING PAUL

INTRODUCTION

Where did all this madness come from?
E. R. Dodds

Few figures in Western history have been the subject of greater controversy than Saint Paul. Few have caused more dissension and hatred. None has suffered more misunderstanding at the hands of both friends and enemies. None has produced more animosity between Jews and Christians. Typical are the sentiments of Friedrich Nietzsche, contrasting Paul to Jesus:

> The "glad tidings" [of Jesus] were followed closely by the absolutely *worst* tidings—those of St. Paul. Paul is the incarnation of a type which is the reverse of that of the Saviour; he is the genius in hatred, in the standpoint of hatred, and in the relentless logic of hatred. And alas what did this dysevangelist not sacrifice to his hatred. . . . He

> did more: he once more falsified the history of Israel, so
> as to make it appear as a prologue to *his* mission.[1]

Nietzsche is correct on several counts. First, Paul has long been regarded as the source for Christian hatred of Jews and Judaism. Second, among Jews he has been the most hated of all Christians. And third, the issue of Paul's conversion—for Nietzsche, his hallucination—lies at the center of all debates about the apostle.

Little wonder that Paul has raised vexing questions across almost twenty centuries. How did this zealous Jew, Saul the Pharisee, who by his own admission had been an active persecutor, a hater, of the early Jesus-movement, suddenly emerge as a fervent follower of the risen Jesus? How are we to understand his role as the apostle of Jesus Christ to the Gentiles in relation to this dramatic transformation? Should we think of him as a religious convert? If so, from what to what? Did the apostle to the Gentiles turn his back on his former life as a Jew and become the spokesman for early Christian anti-Judaism? Did he carry forward his hatred and transfer it to his former faith? How did this feisty preacher-organizer, bitterly attacked and hated in his own time by other apostles within the Jesus-movement and labeled the apostle of the heretics by a mainstream Christian writer as late as the end of the second century C.E., eventually come to be installed at the very heart of the Christian scriptures, the New Testament?

Not surprisingly, given both the dramatic turn of events in his own life and the efforts by later Christians of every conceivable stripe to claim him as "their" apostle, it has proven exceedingly difficult to pin down the real Paul, to free him from the clutches of his many friends and enemies. Only one set of issues has yielded anything like a consensus among readers of Paul, including his friends (those who claimed to be his true followers) as well as his enemies (those who reviled him for his apparent hostility toward the law):[2]

- He was a convert from Judaism to Christianity.

- His role as apostle to the Gentiles caused him to turn against his former life.

- As a Christian apostle he repudiated the law of Moses, the Torah, and circumcision, not just for Gentiles but for Jews as well.

- The law had never been intended by God as the path to salvation, for Gentiles or Jews.

- The Jews, having turned their back on Jesus as their Messiah, had now been rejected by God as a disobedient people and been replaced by Gentiles as the new people of God. Israel has stumbled and failed by virtue of its refusal to accept Paul's gospel.

- Paul thus stands as the father of Christian anti-Judaism, the theologian of the rejection-replacement view.

- Paul was installed at the center of the New Testament precisely because he, like the later Christian communities that shaped these Christian scriptures and produced the New Testament, shared their rejection-replacement view of Judaism.

- All of this is clearly laid out in his letters.

Despite the reigning consensus on these issues, it has long been recognized that it contains major difficulties. For on every one of these statements, Paul's letters offer up totally contradictory evidence. To illustrate these contradictions, I put forward two sets of texts, drawn from his letters. I will label one set anti-Israel, or anticircumcision, or antilaw; the other, I will label pro-Israel, procircumcision, or prolaw.

The Anti-Israel Set

- "For all who rely on works of the law are under a curse" (Gal. 3.10).

- "Now it is evident that no man is justified before God by the law" (Gal. 3.11).

- "For neither circumcision counts for anything, nor uncircumcision, but a new creation" (Gal. 6.15).

- "For no human being will be justified in his sight by works of the law, since through the law comes knowledge of sin" (Rom. 3.20).

- "Israel who pursued righteousness which is based on the law did not succeed in fulfilling that law" (Rom. 9.31).

- "As regards the gospel, they are enemies of God, for your sake" (Rom. 11.28).

- "But their minds were hardened; for to this day, when they read the old covenant, that same veil remains unlifted, because only through Christ is it taken away. Yes, to this day, whenever Moses is read a veil lies over their mind; but when a man turns to the Lord the veil is removed" (2 Cor. 3.14f.).

The Pro-Israel Set

- "What is the advantage of the Jew? Or what is the value of circumcision? Much in every way" (Rom. 3.1).

- "Do we overthrow the law through faith? By no means. On the contrary, we uphold the law" (Rom. 3.31).

- "What shall we say? That the law is sin? By no means" (Rom. 7.7).

- "Thus the law is holy, and the commandment is holy and just and good" (Rom. 7.12).

- "To the Israelites belong the sonship, the glory, the covenants, the giving of the law, the Temple, and the promises. To them belong the patriarchs and of their race, according to the flesh, is the Christ" (Rom. 9.4).

- "Has god rejected his people? By no means" (Rom. 11.1).

- "All Israel will be saved" (Rom. 11.26).

- "Is the law then against the promises of God. Certainly not!" (Gal. 3.21).

Now suddenly the problem emerges. Point by point, the two sets appear to contradict each other: Circumcision is of great value; it counts for nothing. The law is holy; it places its followers under a curse and cannot justify them before God. All Israel will be saved; they are the enemies of God and have failed to fulfill their own law.

Here is a major dilemma for all readers of Paul. No one wants an apostle riddled with contradictions. Although some simply ignore the problem, most intelligent readers (I will call them contradictionists) recognize and admit the tensions between the two sets of passages. Among contradictionist readers, one finds four basic techniques for resolving these tensions: psychology, resignation, radical elimination, and subordination.

The psychological technique holds that Paul was lost in a hopeless, if understandable quagmire of intellectual and emotional inconsistency. The ex-Pharisee sought to have it both ways, having abandoned the law but not prepared to admit it. Wishing to maintain an emotional identification with his people, even while adopting positions utterly at odds with that loyalty. Simply unwilling to face the radical consequences of his own thinking, namely, that the law really was obsolete, that circumcision really was of no value, and that being a Jew no longer counted for anything. The contradictory passages are thus assigned to opposite poles of his anguished psyche—the anti-Israel statements reflecting his "real" views as a Christian convert, the pro-Israel statements preserving his unresolved and yet-to-be-discarded loyalties as a Jew. Robert Hamerton-Kelly writes that Paul held onto "the role of Israel in the plan of salvation" due to "powerful personal factors" and to "a case of nostalgia overwhelming his judgment."[3] Similarly, Heikki Räisänen speculates that Paul's ambiguities derived from the fact that he had broken with the law but could not bring himself to admit it.[4]

The resigned technique simply leaves the contradictions as they stand, a position especially prominent in the recent work of Räisänen. "Paul's thought on the law is full of difficulties and inconsistencies."[5] One consequence of this technique, and thus a significant handicap for most Christians, is that his thought is held to be of little theological value for Christians in their relations to Jews. Paul's thinking is so muddled that it yields no useful guidelines. Curiously, this attitude reaches back all the way to the ancient world, if not to Paul's own lifetime. One New Testament writing (2 Peter, dating from around 100 C.E.) speaks of Paul's letters as containing *dusnoêta*, a term that closely approximates Räisänen's "difficulties and inconsistencies." A pagan critic of the third century C.E. accused him of "variable and contradictory utterance."[6] Later still, the enormously influential Christian preacher and writer of the late fourth century John Chrysostom took it on himself to defend the apostle from charges of heresy and inconsistency.[7]

By far the most radical technique is to remove the offending passages altogether. Typical of this approach is J. C. O'Neill's treatment of Romans and Galatians, both of which he assumes to have been expanded, and corrupted, by later editors. Of Romans, O'Neill writes that its thought is "so obscure, so complicated, so disjointed, that it is hard to see how Paul could have exerted such an influence on his contemporaries" if we assume that its preserved form represents his real thinking.[8] And of Galatians he writes: "if Paul was 'a coherent, argumentative, pertinent writer' (Locke), Galatians . . . cannot have been written by Paul."[9] And so he proceeds to eliminate extensive passages on the grounds that they originated among post-Pauline, even un-Pauline, commentators. "If the choice lies between supposing that Paul was confused and contradictory and supposing that his text has been commented on and enlarged, I have no hesitation in choosing the second."[10]

The fourth and final technique, also the dominant one, has been to subordinate one set of passages—always the pro-Israel set—to the other, leaving the anti-Israel version as the true Paul. For those who subscribe to the view of Paul as the father of Christian anti-Judaism, the pro-Israel passages must be explained away. This "subordinationist" technique will occupy the lion's share of this book.

It is clear that we cannot dismiss contradictionist readers out of hand. They have not invented the "difficulties and inconsistencies," the *dusnoêta*, in the Pauline letters. The two sets of passages (pro- and anti-Israel) cannot be ignored. At the same time, however, the solutions offered by the contradictionists betray a certain weakness of will, a readiness to abandon hard thinking, and an inclination to read Paul in settings far removed from his own time and place. Why is it, we must ask, that subordinationist readers always place the ultimate weight on the anti-Israel passages, as if they gave the final word, while treating the pro-Israel passages as inconsistent? What would happen, for example, if we began with the pro-Israel set and worked in the other direction?

Until recently, few have accepted John Chrysostom's challenge to locate the difficulties of Paul's letters not in him but in his readers. Few have asked whether it might be possible to hold, against his ancient and modern critics, that on these fundamental issues Paul was "not variable, but uniform and clear".[11] Is it possible to construct a "uniform and clear" picture of Paul's teachings about the law and Israel, without convicting him of contradictory thinking, but at the same time doing full justice to the two set of passages?

I believe not only that such a picture is possible but that it is the only picture that makes sense of what we know about Paul, his letters, and his times. Focusing on the pro-Israel passages, I will argue that Paul need not, indeed cannot, be read according to the contradictionists and that he is entirely innocent of all charges lodged against him by his critics:

- He is not the father of Christian anti-Judaism.

- He was not the inventor of the rejection-replacement theory.

- He did not repudiate the law of Moses.

- He did not argue that God had rejected Israel.

- His enemies were not Jews outside the Jesus-movement but competing apostles within.

- He did not expect Jews to find their salvation through Jesus Christ.

Beyond this, I will contend that he was acutely aware of misreadings of his views and that he strove mightily to correct them.

Obviously this will not be an easy task. Standing against me are not merely twenty centuries of reading Paul as the father of Christian anti-Judaism, but the manifest tensions between the two sets of texts themselves. But the tide has begun to turn. No longer is the old, traditional view taken for granted. Many readers of Paul—Jews, Christians, and others—not only question the old view but marvel that it ever came to be in the first place. But before we can accept this challenge, we need to exercise caution on several fronts.

First, we can never penetrate behind his words to his inner thoughts or his "real" intentions. We have only his words and can never be confident that they perfectly translate his intentions.[12] I happen to believe that there is, at least sometimes, a significant congruence between words and intentions, but I cannot prove this. In any case, dealing with the words alone is already a difficult task, as we shall see.

Second, we can never be certain that Paul's words conveyed to his readers what he wanted to communicate. Indeed, I will argue that his letter to the Romans represents an extended effort by the apostle to correct certain fundamental misunderstandings of his position on Israel and the law. Thus we will need to pay close attention to readers, ancient and modern. How have they read Paul's words? What assumptions have they brought with them? What has inclined all these readers to interpret Paul's letters in one way rather than another? In other words, it will be a fundamental contention of this book that the meaning of a text—a letter, a poem, a commentary—never arises from the text in isolation but instead in a dynamic interaction between readers and the text. Put differently, meaning is never governed by the words of the text alone but is created in the act of responding to them by real persons in concrete circumstances and contexts.[13]

Third, having already noted the apparent inconsistencies between the two sets of passages previously cited, we must resist the temptation to rescue Paul from the embarrassment of contradiction and inconsistency by engaging in tortured exegesis. We need to be able to admit, in the end, that he was self-contradictory, inconsistent, unclear, irrelevant, and even wrong. But the words *in the end* are important. For I am convinced that we are justified in pronouncing such judgments only as a last resort. The danger that must be overcome is cultural myopia, the all-too-familiar tendency to label something as inconsistent or irrational simply because it fails to follow our way of thinking or because we have not plunged deeply enough into the circumstances surrounding the original author and readers. Only when we have tried, and failed, to make sense of a text in its own time and place can we throw up our arms and proclaim, "This really makes no sense!"

Fourth, we need to recognize that in dealing with Paul we are faced with an enormous cultural artifact. The persons and parties who put together the New Testament gave him pride of place —of the twenty-seven writings in that collection, more than half (fourteen to be precise) were written by him, or were attributed to him, or are about him (Acts), while two others (2 Peter and James) clearly show his influence. As a collection, the New Testament was created long after Paul's death, and we cannot assume that the Paul of the New Testament is the same as the

Paul of his own Romans or Galatians. Better yet, we know that they were not the same. In the decades and centuries following his death, there were many Pauls—the Paul of Acts, of Ephesians, of the Pastoral Epistles (1–2 Timothy and Titus), of Marcion, of Valentinus,[14] of the Acts of Paul,[15] of the Jewish Christian groups who reviled him as an apostle of Satan, and so on.[16] Indeed, so many different Christian groups claimed his authority and read his texts that the second-century Christian writer Tertullian could refer to him, with a heavy dose of irony, as "the apostle of the heretics." Among these heretics was the second century figure of Marcion, who likely produced the first version of the New Testament and who advanced an extreme version of Christian anti-Judaism, all of this in Paul's name.

Eventually Marcion's efforts were rejected by mainstream Christianity. But an anti-Jewish Paul was the price paid for rescuing the apostle from Marcion and his kind. In other words, not only has Paul (not the "historical" Paul but his letters with their later misinterpretations) exercised an immeasurable impact on Western history and thought, but he has always been the focus of bitter controversy. He comes to us with a history and a reputation. We need to know something of both or risk being captured by them. There is no neutral ground on which to meet him. What, we need to ask, were the views about the law, Israel, and the Jews among the persons and parties who created the New Testament, with Paul at its center?

Fifth, we need to learn to read Paul as his earliest readers would have responded to him and, presumably, as Paul himself would have wished. Critics have long commented that Paul's letters reveal a sophisticated use of rhetorical devices familiar to educated writers and readers in the Greco-Roman world. But seldom have these observations been put to use in interpreting his thoughts; instead they have tended to focus on matters of style. Rhetorical training, for instance, encouraged writers to introduce other voices, to shift audiences, even to put forward contradictory views in competing voices. Obviously, such devices create problems for the modern reader, unaccustomed to the fluid dynamics of ancient rhetoric. The words are Paul's, but whose is the voice? How can we detect irony or hyperbole? At times, Paul indicates explicitly that he has shifted audience and is addressing a fictitious person within the letter (e.g., Rom. 2.1—"Therefore you are without any defense, my friend (*anthrôpe*)"). But elsewhere he is more subtle; we need to pay close attention to dramatic shifts of voice. The recent works of Stanley Stowers[17] and John Lodge[18] have demonstrated how a rhetorical reading of Paul can take us in radically new directions. Their work has revealed a new law: *If you miss Paul's rhetorical strategies, you will get him wrong.*[19]

Sixth, we need to recognize the extent to which modern translations, dictionaries, and commentaries are embedded within preexisting interpretations. The original Greek text (the autograph as it left the hand of Paul's scribe, as well as all early copies) consisted of an unbroken series of letters—no spaces between words, no punctuation, no verses, and no chapters. The much later imposition of verses and chapters reflects entrenched ways of understanding Paul's letters. They are not innocent conveniences. They need to be regarded with suspicion. Speaking of the chapter divisions at Romans 2.1 and 4.1, Stowers insists that "the standard textual arrangement has completely obscured Paul's rhetoric."[20] Similarly with translations. They too need to be regarded with suspicion. Paul Meyer speaks tellingly of crucial exegetical decisions "made on grounds extrinsic to the text itself."[21] The same can be said of many translations. Lloyd Gaston sighs, "I find that I cannot trust even such 'objective' works as lexica on some points."[22]

At this point, the basic issues are beginning to come into sharper focus:

1. On certain questions—questions central to Romans and Galatians—Paul's words seem inconsistent, even contradictory. These questions concern the law (of Moses), including circumcision, and its continued validity after the coming of Jesus Christ.

2. These tensions have traditionally been resolved in a number of ways, generally by ignoring the pro-Israel texts altogether or by subordinating them to the anti-Israel texts, arguing that the latter tell the real story. In accordance with this view, Romans and Galatians must be read as a sustained polemic against Judaism and against the law, insisting that it had never been intended as the path to salvation for Gentiles or Jews, that it led to sin, and that it was incapable of being followed in any case. Only by reading Paul in this manner can he emerge as the originator and most articulate spokesman for the rejection-replacement view of Judaism, that is, that the Jews, the old people of God, along with the old law have been rejected by God and replaced by a new people (Christians, a term never used by Paul).

3. This rejection-replacement view of Judaism quickly became the dominant stance within Christian circles in the early centuries; it underlies the message and structure of the New Testament as a whole. And it is within this structure that Paul stands as the central figure. For the New Testament and certainly for those who created it, Paul was *the* theologian of Christian anti-Judaism, the rejection-replacement view of Judaism. Virtually all later readers—Christian, Jewish, and other— have assumed that Paul stands behind the anti-Judaism of the New Testament and mainstream Christianity. "It is Paul who has provided the theoretical structure for Christian anti-Judaism from Marcion through Luther and F. C. Baur down to Bultmann."[23]

4. This view of Paul—I call it the old, the traditional, the standard view—has remained dominant until very recent times, when it has been called into question from a number of angles. Some, as we have seen, contend that he was simply confused and unable to make up his mind. Others, most notably E. P. Sanders, have insisted that Paul never argued that there was anything wrong with Judaism, just that it had been superseded by Christianity. In a memorable line, Sanders sums up this posi-

tion: "In short, *this is what Paul finds wrong in Judaism: it is not Christianity.*"[24] But for Sanders, it remains true that Paul "*explicitly denies that the Jewish covenant can be effective for salvation, thus consciously denying the basis of Judaism.*"[25]

Still others, beginning with Krister Stendahl (1963)[26] and reaching from Lloyd Gaston (1977) to Stanley Stowers (1994), John Lodge (1996), and others, have taken an altogether different tack, arguing not only (with Sanders) that Paul never argues against the law but further that he never espouses the rejection-replacement at all (against Sanders and many others). Indeed, that he argues strenuously and repeatedly against it. This position holds that the traditional view is mistaken, not just in this or that detail but in every respect, from top to bottom.

In making my case, I will look first at the traditional view, considering both Christian and Jewish readers (Chapter 1) who see in Paul the origins of Christian anti-Judaism.[27] Among Jewish readers in particular we will find that Paul's seeming rejection of the Jewish law is often accompanied by the claim that he profoundly misunderstood the essentials of Judaism or, alternatively, that his perception of the law was distorted by a heavy dose of Greek culture. In a few cases, however, Christian and Jewish readers have insisted that even Paul's rejection of the law can be understood entirely in Jewish terms and that he remained a Jew in every respect.

In seeking to understand the origins and the remarkable persistence of the traditional view (Chapter 2) we will need to consider a wide range of topics: his conversion or commission to be an apostle of Christ; his troubled career as an apostle; the role of his letters in the New Testament and their influence on later Christian theology; and, most of all, the interpretive assumptions of modern critics. Some might argue that it is self-defeating to give so much attention to views that one is seeking to undermine. But it is not enough just to put forward a new position, especially a radical one; in addition, one needs to make an effort to explain where the old position came from, how it went wrong and why it managed to dominate the scene for so long.

In presenting the new view (Chapter 3), in its several forms, I will stress the fundamental contributions of Stendahl, Gaston, and Stowers. At the same time, I will attempt to show, as one critic puts it, that "a major shift seems to be taking place in Pauline studies, a shift that some would even call a revolution."[28] In line with this shift has come an inclination to question everything in the old paradigm. Among proponents of the new paradigm one finds a characteristic sense of dismay at how the old model came to be in the first place and of disbelief at how it could have survived so long, given that it is so obviously wrong.[29] "I suddenly find that I have great difficulty in reading the standard literature on Paul: why do other interpreters miss the obvious while spending much time on matters not in the text at all?"[30] I must emphasize, however, that this new view is still very much in the minority. Although it has attracted a greater following than was the case twenty years ago, it is still revolutionary in content rather than popularity. Finally, I will examine the two letters of Paul where issues of the law, the Jews, and the new dispensation of Jesus Christ occupy center stage: Galatians (Chapter 4) and Romans (Chapter 5).

Overall, my argument will be heavily contextual—that is, I will insist that the old view of Paul arose from reading him in alien, remote contexts (i.e., those of later Christianity). And I will justify the new view by arguing that we must read him within contexts that place us closer to his time and place. Specifically, these contexts will be (1) Paul's activity within the early Jesus-movement, including his mission to the Gentiles and the persistent opposition to that mission from within the movement; (2) his standing within the literary and religious culture of Greco-Roman Judaism; and (3) his use of Greco-Roman rhetoric in addressing his Gentile communities. In general, my contention will be that unless a reading of Paul makes sense within these three contexts it cannot be taken seriously. Typical of this new image is Stowers's picture of a re-Judaized Paul:

> This Paul seems plausible as a former Pharisee. Paul
> fully accepted the temple and other Jewish institutions,
> although he, like most other Jews, may have at times
> criticized their current administration by those who were
> in power. Paul most distanced himself from other forms
> of Judaism in his devotion to Jesus Christ. . . . The apos-
> tle was nonetheless as fully monotheistic as other Jews; and
> not monotheistic as monotheism was radically redefined
> by orthodox Christianity.[31]

Before proceeding to the heart of the matter, I need to say a
word or two about what is at stake for me in this project. Why
another book on Paul? What difference does it make whether
one chooses the old view or the new? As for myself, I have no
particular religious or theological view to defend.[32] I am Christian
only in the broad cultural sense of that word; I am affiliated with
no religious institution of any kind. At the same time, I am not
so naive as to believe that I have no interest in the outcome of
this debate or that I stand on neutral ground. Nonetheless, my
involvement in this project is largely intellectual. But to say intellectual is not to deny my passion for the issues at stake. The new
view has enthralled me for a number of years; it has tested my
intellectual and moral fiber. The effort to comprehend a dominant paradigm, to move beyond it, and to construct a new one
has given me more sheer intellectual joy than I can possibly communicate. But again, so what? What does it matter beyond my
personal horizons? As one critic of my earlier work has complained,
"Paul himself may bear less of the responsibility for this sad story
[of Christian anti-Semitism] than earlier writers have claimed,
but in all honesty it must be said that this consideration seems
merely antiquarian." And he continues, "To avoid having
Gager's premises lead to this conclusion [that Paul held the Jews
to be foolish at the very least], one would have to claim that Paul
considers the Jews still *obliged* to maintain Torah. . . . Even Gager
cannot extend his rereading of Paul quite that far; he does not
even try."[33]

As for the second point, this is precisely the view I wish to maintain—that Paul considers the Jews still obligated to maintain the Torah and that he says so explicitly (e.g., Rom. 3.1–2: "What is the advantage of the Jew? Or what is the value of circumcision? Much in every way!"; Gal. 5.3; cf. 5.11: "I testify again to every man who receives circumcision that he is obliged to keep the whole law."). Indeed, this is the only view that makes sense of his repeated argument that his gospel to the Gentiles is fully articulated in the Torah. As one Jewish critic has insisted, "It is quite clear . . . that both factions [of the Jesus-movement] in Jerusalem agreed that Jews, even after Jesus, remained under the prescriptions of the Torah."[34]

On the first charge, that textual study amounts to little more than antiquarianism, I plead both guilty and innocent. Guilty in that my fundamental concern is historical and that my primary goal is to get it right, to argue that the traditional view of Paul is wrong, not just here and there but from start to finish, and to convince others of my case. At the same time, I plead innocent because I believe that our history, or rather what we think and know of it, does matter in the present. I would not claim that Paul, or even Christianity as a whole, is responsible for modern anti-Semitism. But Paul in the traditional reading has been an important part of that story. If that version should turn out to be wrong, the story will need to be revised. "[M]uch is at stake here. Jews cannot view with much sympathy a Christianity that adheres to the teaching of contempt for the Torah of Moses."[35] Conversely, from a Christian perspective, "a Christian church with an anti-semitic New Testament is abominable."[36]

By now it should be obvious that I advocate a new reading of Paul not simply as one possible alternative, as one contender alongside others, but as the only historically defensible one. This is a bold stance, perhaps even foolish. It is certainly out of step with modern theories that regard all views as possible and allow no ultimate adjudication among them. It is also highly presumptuous, even arrogant, in its insistence that twenty centuries and most readers of Paul have been utterly mistaken, and in demanding that they confront the sources of that mistake. Put differently, if the old view of Paul should prove to be untenable, all readers, Jewish as well as Christian, will need to confront the reasons for its origins in the past and its remarkable persistence through twenty centuries.

CHAPTER ONE

THE TRADITIONAL VIEW OF PAUL

"It was Paul who delivered the Christian religion from Judaism. . . .
It was he who confidently regarded the Gospel as a new force
abolishing the religion of the law."
Adolf Harnack

THE ELEMENTS OF THE TRADITIONAL VIEW

These words of the German historian Adolf Harnack summarize the traditional view of Paul: his gospel stands in opposition to the law; his Christianity is the antithesis of Judaism.[1] Underlying this view are several additional claims that provide its essential foundations:

- Paul underwent a typical conversion from one religion to another, in this case from Judaism to Christianity.

- As a result of this conversion, he preached against the Jewish law, against Judaism, and against Israel. The content of this negative teaching was that the law, the old covenant with Israel (essentially what Christians came to call the Old Testament), was no longer the path to salvation, for Jews or Gentiles; indeed God had never intended it to be; and that God had rejected the Jews/Israel as the chosen people.

- At the same time the radical antithesis between Judaism and Christianity is represented as a decisive transition from religious particularism to religious universalism.

- Most interpreters insist that Paul's polemic against the law is founded on a sound understanding of ancient Judaism.

- Others argue that his views reveal profound misunderstandings and distortions.

- In either case, there remains a deep ambivalence as to whether Paul the convert can in any way be understood against the background of ancient Judaism. Paul transcended Judaism.

Paul Converted from Judaism to Christianity

Essential to the traditional view is the image of Paul the convert.[2] Or better yet, since interpreters have rarely bothered to consider the variety or the dynamics of conversions, one particular type of conversion is invoked, the sudden movement from one religion to another. Within this one subtype of conversion, there is yet another unexamined assumption, namely, that Paul's conversion to a new religion resulted in the repudiation of his former one. In a word, Paul converted from Judaism to Christianity and as a consequence denied all validity to the former.

There is no denying that Paul underwent a significant change of heart at some point in his life and that this change led him in fundamentally new directions.[3] It is also true that he uses language reminiscent of conversion experiences from other times and places. In his letter to the Philippians, where he is forced to defend the legitimacy of his own apostolic status against other apostles within the Jesus-movement, he first boasts of his Jewish credentials (3.5–6): "circumcised on the eighth day, of the people of Israel, of the tribe of Benjamin, a Hebrew born of Hebrews, as to the law a Pharisee, as to zeal a persecutor of the church, as to righteousness under the law blameless." But then, in a sudden turnabout, he proclaims,

> Whatever gain I had, I counted as loss for the sake of Christ. Indeed, I count everything as loss because of the surpassing worth of knowing Christ Jesus my Lord. For his sake I have suffered the loss of all things and count them as rubbish in order that I may gain Christ and be found in him, not having my righteousness from the law/Torah, but from the faithfulness of Christ (3.8–9).[4]

This sounds like the language of a convert.[5] But of what sort? From what to what? Does he generalize from his own experience? Are there common threads in his life before and after the turnabout? Can we make use of the three accounts of Paul's conversion, his Damascus Road experience as reported in the Book of Acts (9.1–9; 22.6–16; 26.12–18)?

It is difficult to know where to begin in unraveling the tangled web of unexamined assumptions at work among those who assume that Paul converted from Judaism to Christianity. Most problematic of all is the use of the term *Christianity* by almost everyone.[6] Paul himself never uses the term in any form. Is it too much to insist that since he failed to use the term he may not have had any notion of a new religion as the term Christianity implies? The use of Christianity is typical of a persistent trend in Pauline studies—to complete his sentences for him, to supply missing words, and to make explicit what he leaves unspoken. Consider Alan Segal's comment on Romans 11.26: "Paul, however, does not draw a detailed picture of what he envisions at the end of time, when some of Israel will embrace Christianity."[7]

What Paul says, however, is somewhat different: "and so all Israel will be saved."

Much more serious than introducing words and thoughts not used by Paul are the consequences of these supplements. Some readers pay lip service to the idea that Paul (not to mention Jesus and the early Jesus-movement in its entirety) had no notion of Christianity or, for that matter, of themselves as constituting a new religion. Most ignore the issue altogether. Both continue to use the term as if it made no difference. But it does matter. Words do things. They are embedded in networks of meaning and carry these meanings with them wherever they go. In our Western lexicon, Christian signifies, among other things, "not Jewish/Israel," "different from Jewish/Israel," even "against Jewish/Israel." Thus when we use phrases like Paul's Christianity or Paul's Gentile Christian believers, we prejudge, and thus bypass, certain fundamental questions. To speak of Paul's Christianity implies that he thought of himself as fundamentally different from, even opposed to Jews/Israel. The term is not only anachronistic;[8] it is misleading. It is embedded in the tradition that sees Christianity as outside, even opposed to Judaism, and its use reinforces and presupposes that tradition. The only sensible position is stated by a recent Jewish reader, Pinchas Lapide: "Paul did not become a Christian, since there were no Christians in those times."[9] Paul knows only two categories of human beings—Jews (he also uses Israel) and Gentiles (*ta ethnê*; he also speaks of Greeks). To import the category of Christian is to violate his thought-world and impose an alien concept.

From the moment we begin to speak of Christianity in Paul, the conversion issue is settled. Paul became a Christian! And he repudiated Judaism. But if he had no concept of Christianity or of Christians, if there was no Christianity, this cannot be the case. He became something else: the apostle to the Gentiles!

There are other problems with the standard model of Paul's conversion. We are familiar with the modern phenomenon of conversion within a religion, from one type of Christian community to another or from one variety of Judaism to another, with no sense that the convert thereby abandons or repudiates Christianity or Judaism itself.[10] The same holds true of ancient Judaism, when various groups of Jews frequently sought to win other Jews to their point of view.[11] This is a model altogether different from the one that involves movement from one religion to another. In the case of Paul, who never speaks of Christianity and insists that God (and presumably Paul as well) has not rejected Israel, the model of a conversion within a religious tradition is clearly more appropriate than any other.[12] Thus Segal's puzzled comment that Paul became a Christian "but seemed unaware of leaving Judaism" is both misleading and unnecessary.[13] Misleading because it assumes that Paul became a Christian and unnecessary because most converts never leave their religion at all.

At this point we need to step back and ask two questions: what was Paul doing prior to his conversion? And how does he present the conversion in those few additional places where he discusses it?

On the first question, Paul is clear about what his relations with the Jesus movement were before his conversion; he is also deeply troubled by them.[14]

> You have heard of my former behaviour in Judaism, how I persecuted the church of God violently and tried to destroy it; and I advanced in Judaism beyond many of my own age among my people, so extremely zealous was I for the traditions of the fathers. But when he who had set me apart before I was born, and had called me through his grace, was pleased to reveal his Son to me, in order that I might preach him among the Gentiles . . . (Gal. 1.13–16).

What was it that led this zealous Pharisee to persecute the followers of Jesus, to the point of trying to destroy the movement? The recent consensus is that the central issue for Paul was Gentiles and their standing in the Jesus-movement.[15] We know from numerous sources that Gentiles caused deep divisions and disputes within the Jesus-movement and that Paul was a central figure in these controversies. Within the movement, the hotly debated questions were whether Gentile followers of Jesus needed to become Jews, that is, whether male members needed to undergo circumcision. Did Gentile followers need to observe the Torah, the law of Moses? Paul's answer was unequivocal—Gentiles were not required to adopt circumcision or to follow the Jewish law.

We can never know with certainty what led Paul to persecute the church so violently. Some have proposed that it was the very idea of a crucified messiah that was found to be offensive. Others have argued that it was because some followers of Jesus were admitting Gentile believers as Israelites without requiring them to be fully observant of the law. But, as Paula Fredriksen has rightly shown, this may not have been Paul's basis for persecuting the church before his conversion. Perhaps, she suggests, Jews like Paul feared Roman retaliation in response to reports that "the Jewish community harbored messianists from Palestine who spoke of coming battles" against Rome.[16] In the end, all that we can know for certain is that Gentiles constituted the heart of his gospel after his conversion and were probably a central concern before.

Further support for the Gentiles as a lifelong preoccupation derives from the particular conversion-model that Paul's transformation seems to have followed. The model in question here is the "transvaluation/reversal of values," according to which the convert moves from one pole to another of opposing systems, whether religious, political, or other.[17] A radical socialist becomes a radical conservative; a prison guard embraces the worldview of the inmate; a fervent persecutor of a religious movement converts to that very movement. The negative pole becomes positive and vice versa. Typical of this sort of conversion is the language of Phil. 3.7: "Whatever gain I had I counted as loss for the sake of Christ. Indeed, I count everything as loss." What is important to note here is that the convert does not move to something new and unknown but rather to something that already involves a deep emotional and religious engagement, albeit a negative one. The entire system remains intact but is turned upside down. If this is the case, and if Gentiles are found at the center of Paul's world after his conversion, there is every reason to believe that Gentiles stood at the center of his thinking before his conversion. Indeed, Gentiles may well have been the pivot on which the whole system turned. Thus, contrary to the traditional view of Paul's conversion and its consequences, what changed was not his view of the law as such, or of the law in relation to Israel, but only as it concerned Gentiles!

What cannot be denied is that Paul understood the essential content of his conversion to be his mission to the Gentiles. In Romans 11.13 he refers to himself simply as "the apostle to the Gentiles" (*apostolos ethnôn*). That he takes this title and mission to be the direct consequence of his conversion experience is clear not only in Galatians, where he speaks of a revelation "in order that I might preach him among the Gentiles" (1.16) but also in Romans, where he presents himself as having received "grace and apostleship to bring about the obedience of faith for the sake of his name among all the Gentiles" (1.5). Again in Romans, he speaks of "the grace given me by God to be a minister of Christ Jesus to the Gentiles" (15.15–16). In other words, Paul's apostleship, his conversion, centered on his gospel to the Gentiles.

Paul Preached against the Law and Israel

The claim that Paul preached against the law and Israel stands as the central feature in the traditional view of Paul. His conversion turned him against the law: the law was no longer, indeed never had been, the means of Israel's justification or redemption; the law led to a knowledge of sin; the law ended in condemnation; the sole path to salvation, for Gentiles and Jews, leads through Jesus Christ; neither Jews nor Gentiles can or should observe anything of the old law; circumcision was of no value; Israel has been rejected by God, and so on.

By now it should be clear that there are many problems with this view. First, Paul explicitly denies every one of these statements (see the pro-Israel set of passages above). But he also says things that sound very much like the traditional Paul. We have just noted, however, that as the apostle to the Gentiles Paul may not having been speaking of Israel at all in these perhaps mislabeled anti-Israel passages. We will need to consider this possibility at greater length.

We have already seen that the tensions between the traditional image of Paul and the pro-Israel passages have confronted readers with an unhappy dilemma. How can the apostle be rescued from self-contradiction? For some, the solution is simple. They simply ignore the pro-Israel passages. But for serious readers this will not do. They look elsewhere. Typical is the argument that Romans 11.1 ("Has God rejected his people? By no means!") refers to Paul himself, a Jew, and other Jews, like Peter, who have come to believe in Jesus Christ. This is the remnant theory according to which God's promise to redeem his people is reconciled with the rejection of Israel by pointing to the small number of Jews who "converted" to faith in Jesus Christ. But what of Rom. 11.26 ("All Israel will be saved") that speaks neither of conversion nor of a remnant?[18] This is a problem.

One way of handling this problem is to dwell on defects of Paul's thinking—he was either incapable of systematic, consistent thought or unable to follow the implications of his own views to their logical conclusion. This first group of Paul's "contradictionist" critics take the recurrent inconsistencies as a given. "Paul's confused and often inconsistent reasoning, with its various gaps and omissions, is inclined to bore us."[19] "The letter to the Romans comes as near being a theological treatise as anything which Paul wrote—and causes one to give thanks that he wrote no other."[20] Paul's logic is "capricious," his arguments amount to "arbitrary interpretations and fantasies," and his view of the law in Galatians is an "infantile absurdity."[21] "It is no great feat to unearth contradictions, even among his leading thoughts."[22] "I can see only one way: contradictions and tensions have to be *accepted* as *constant* features of Paul's theology."[23]

Responses to these contradictionist critics vary widely. Some seek to turn Paul's defects into virtues, claiming that he was more of a poet;[24] an existentialist ahead of his time;[25] a mystic;[26] or a Semitic thinker who reveled in paradox.[27] Another solution seeks to dissolve the apparent contradictions by assigning them to different periods in the apostle's life.[28]

One common solution has been to deflect attention from the apparent tensions in Paul's thought by focusing instead on the reasons for his rejection of the law and Israel. This solution resembles that of the contradictionists in taking the rejection of the law for granted. But unlike the contradictionists, these readers put aside the pro-Israel texts and concentrate on Paul's difficulties with the law. Various reasons are given for these difficulties. One explanation holds that as a Pharisee, even before his conversion, he had experienced the law as an unbearable burden and found himself unable to live up to its demands. Thus the idea of redemption through Christ, without the law, relieved him of a crippling sense of guilt.[29] This explanation places great emphasis on Romans 7.22–23, in which Paul appears to articulate the impossibility of upholding the law ("I delight in the law of God, in my inmost self, but I see in my members another law at war with the law of my mind and making me captive to the law of sin"). But today hardly any serious reader takes the passage as autobiographical.[30]

Another reason sometimes given is that Paul, while still a Pharisee, came to see that the law was inextricably connected to sin, even the cause of sin. The "negative" passages in Romans (e.g., 7.7: "If it had not been for the law, I would not have known sin") and Galatians (e.g., 3.19–20: "Why, then, the law? It was added because of transgressions . . .") are taken as indicating that he had dramatically revised his evaluation of the law as a positive expression of God's will. We should note, however, that in both letters he appears to take pains to head off this sort

of misreading; cf. Gal. 3.21: "Is the law then against the promises of God? Certainly not!" and Romans 7.7: "What shall we
say? That the law is sin? By no means!" But for most readers, ancient
as well as modern, these warnings appear to have been given
in vain.

A third explanation is that Paul the convert came to see the
law as the source of Israel's unjustified religious and ethnic
exclusivism, as manifested in the insistence that Gentiles had
to accept Judaism in order to be righteous. Thus, according to
James D. G. Dunn, the apostle to the Gentiles "was not against
the law as such—far less against 'good works'! What he aimed
his arguments against was *the law understood and practiced in
such a way as to limit the grace of God, to prevent Gentiles as
Gentiles enjoying it in full measure.*"[31] And, adds Dunn, "*it was Paul
who effectively undermined this third pillar of second Temple
Judaism.*"[32]

A final claim, similar in some respects to the previous one, is
that Paul abandons Judaism because of its religious particularism and embraces, or perhaps creates the religious universalism
of Christianity. Although its roots lie deep in the Christian
tradition, this position reached its classic formulation in the
work of the nineteenth-century church historian F. C. Baur:

> Thus not only was he [Paul] the first to lay down
> expressly and distinctly the principle of Christian uni-
> versalism as a thing essentially opposed to Jewish par-
> ticularism. . . . We cannot call his conversion . . . anything
> but a miracle; and the miracle appears all the greater when
> we remember that in this revulsion of his consciousness
> he broke through the barriers of Judaism and rose out of
> the particularism of Judaism into the universal idea of
> Christianity.[33]

Following Baur, some Christian readers, like Harnack and Ernst
Käsemann, have seen this shift as positive;[34] for others, like Nils
Dahl, it is negative, or rather historically inaccurate and theologically

incorrect. Dahl speaks of the need

> to break radically with the common but simplistic notion
> of a contrast between Christian universalism and Jewish
> particularism. Jewish monotheism at the time of Paul was
> universalistic in its way and Christian monotheism
> remained exclusive. . . . We would come closer to the truth
> by saying that both Jewish and Christian monotheism are
> particular as well as universal, specific as well as general.[35]

More recently, a perceptive Jewish reader of Paul, Daniel Boyarin, has taken up this theme again, arguing that Paul's cultural critique of Judaism, inspired by his immersion in Platonic philosophy, took the form of a "passionate desire for human unification."[36] But, like others, Boyarin hesitates in the end, uncertain whether to attribute the denigration of "carnal Israel" to Paul or to his successors. "Paul had (almost against his will) sown the seeds for a Christian discourse that would completely deprive Jewish ethnic, cultural identity of any positive value."[37]

Paul Understood the Judaism He Criticized and Rejected

The issue here is twofold: first, Paul the Pharisee fully understood Judaism and criticized it on the basis of his new religious understanding; and second, the Judaism criticized by Paul is reconstructed largely from a reading of Paul's letters, a reading based on the assumption that his letters talk about Judaism! This is an obviously vicious circle.

On the first issue, as we have just seen, first-century Judaism is regularly described, using Paul as the primary evidence, as a religion of narrow ethnic interests; as a piety, particularly in its Pharisaic and later Rabbinic forms, of dry, legalist religion in which individuals earned their way to salvation (works righteousness); or, alternatively, as a faith of impossible demands (the law) and harsh judgments (no forgiveness). Other elements can be added: the Jewish god was too remote; Judaism outside of Palestine had sold out to Greek influences; and so on. On every point, Judaism stands in sharp contrast to Christianity. A classic version of this portrait appears in Rudolf Bultmann's *Primitive Christianity in Its Contemporary Setting*. His chapter entitled "Jewish Legalism" offers the following portrait of the Pharisees (Paul's own party):

> ... that sanctity was an entirely negative affair, since most of the regulations were negative and prohibitive in character.... To take them seriously meant making life an intolerable burden. It was almost impossible to *know* the rules, let alone put them into practice.[38]

The notion of Judaism, in its entirety, as a religion of works-righteousness, exposed and transcended by Paul, reappears prominently in the work of Ernst Käsemann (a student of Bultmann's), most notably in his influential commentary on Romans. "The obedience of faith abrogates the law as a mediator of salvation, sees through the perversion of understanding it as a principle of achievement."[39] "Failing to understand the law, it [Israel] falls into illusion and is overthrown. Christ exposes the illusion."[40] In short, Paul rightly repudiates the Judaism of his time as a religion of works-righteousness and self-righteousness. But as E. P. Sanders and others before him have repeatedly argued, "The supposed objection to Jewish self-righteousness is as absent from Paul's letters as self-righteousness itself is from Jewish literature."[41]

The other side to this story, the vicious part of the circle, is that the dismal picture of Judaism in Christian history is drawn largely from a misreading of Paul's own letters, rather than from the enormous body of Jewish evidence from the period. George Foote Moore,[42] E. P. Sanders,[43] and Charlotte Klein[44] have each drawn attention to the distorted and profoundly flawed representations of ancient Judaism in Christian scholarship. This is a beast that will not be slain. Like the proverbial phoenix, it constantly reemerges from its own ashes, so deeply is it embedded in the structures of Western civilization.

Less noticed have been the "Pauline" foundations of these structures. A sympathetic Jewish reader of Paul has put it with biting irony:

> He was then certainly not the great pathologist (as Wellhausen calls him) of *Rabbinic* Judaism at all. And this conclusion . . . would be of considerable importance. For the gruesome horrors and the sad, inevitable fiasco of Rabbinic Judaism (with which so many Christian scholars have made us familiar) are mainly drawn from the criticism of Paul. He said so: he had been through the mill, and he ought to know. Doubtless the Rabbinic writings have been made to furnish proof that what Paul said was accurate and right.[45]

Why is it, wonders Pinchas Lapide, that so few readers have failed to see that the traditional Paul "is kicking doors that are already wide open to all biblically knowledgeable Jews."[46]

Paul Misunderstood the Judaism He Criticized and Rejected

Against those who argue that Paul understood the Judaism of his time stand other readers who insist that Paul utterly misunderstood and misrepresented his former faith, George Foote Moore, a liberal Christian, writes as follows:

> How a Jew of Paul's antecedents could ignore, and by implication deny, the great prophetic doctrine of repentance . . . namely, that God, out of love, freely forgives the penitent sinner and restores him to his favor—that seems from a Jewish point of view inexplicable.[47]

Jewish readers have made similar observations. "The Pauline infer-

ence that the law . . . is a law unto death (Rom. 8:2–3; Gal. 3:21)
is one which no Jew could draw."[48] "Here not merely the Old
Testament belief and the living faith of post-Biblical Judaism
are opposed to Paul, but also the Jesus of the Sermon on the
Mount."[49] "Here a faithful Jew can only shake his head in
bewilderment."[50]

There is a curious note in these readers as they face a seeming paradox. How can Paul, the ex-Pharisee, say things about the
law that are completely at odds with everything that we know
about Judaism? Several solutions have been proposed to the paradox. One has been to argue that Paul's conversion led him to
a fundamental reevaluation of the law. Leo Baeck, in a penetrating
essay, "The Faith of Paul," insists that Paul's thought remains Jewish
to the core, emphasizing the notion that in the Messianic era,
at the end of time, the Gentiles would come in and the Torah
would be suspended. "This is Jewish faith, and such was Paul's
faith."[51] But Paul's vision of Christ, his conversion, brought a "turning point in the history of religion . . . a parting of the ways."[52]

Another solution, again popular among Jewish readers, is
that Paul's understanding of Judaism, especially in its Pharisaic
forms, was distorted by his exposure to Greek culture, often with
the implied assertion that "real" Judaism was Pharisaic/Rabbinic
and un-Greek. Paul may well have been a Pharisee, as he claims,
but his education in the Greek city of Tarsus adulterated his grasp
of authentic Judaism.[53]

One final resolution of the paradox, touched on by several critics, but never developed, goes well beyond the conversionist and
the Greek explanations. Moore, after noting the radically un-
Jewish elements of Paul's language, goes on to comment that the
apostle

> was, in fact, not writing to convince Jews but to keep his
> Gentile converts from being convinced by Jewish propa-
> gandists, who insisted that faith in Christ was not suffi-
> cient to salvation apart from observance of the law.[54]

Samuel Sandmel makes a similar observation: "The angry tone of Galatians emerges not because Judaism . . . had infected a church of Paul's own creation, but because Christian Judaizing had infected it . . . the bitter controversies reflected in his Epistles are not with Jews but with [Christian] Judaizers."[55] Even Martin Buber pauses momentarily, after insisting that Paul had opposed the law to faith, to ask, "Or are we to understand by the futile 'works of the Law' merely a performance without faith?"[56] But he fails to exploit his own insight. So, too, Alan Segal speculates that

> it is thus possible that what changes for Paul is merely his view of that medium [the law] of salvation for Gentiles. In other words, Paul may rest all on faith but still maintain the validity of the Jewish faith including the Torah. This would be in keeping with the mature rabbinic view of the second century that salvation for Jew and Gentile alike is based upon righteousness and repentance, and that the ethics by which the Gentiles are judged excludes the special laws that apply to the Jews alone.[57]

With these observations of Moore, Buber, Sandmel, and Segal we find ourselves in new territory. Although none of them seems willing, or able, to carry out the consequences of their insights, they do open a new vista. What they suggest is that it may be possible to answer Moore's (How could Paul ignore the basic tenets of Judaism?) and Schoeps's (How could Paul speak of the law as the cause of death?) questions without resorting either to tortured exegesis or charges of inconsistency. For if Paul, the apostle to the Gentiles, was not writing to Jews but to his own Gentile converts; if he was concerned with the bearing of the law not on Jews but on Gentiles; if his opponents in Galatia and elsewhere were not Jews outside but apostles within the Jesus-movement; if all of this is so, it may be possible not only to dissolve all the contradictions and inconsistencies, along with the supposed polemic against the law and Judaism, but also to restore Paul to his Jewish milieu in a way that takes us several steps beyond even Baeck.

THE ORIGINS OF THE TRADITIONAL VIEW

Before moving to consider the new view of Paul, it seems wise to revisit and expand our grasp of the assumptions that underlie the traditional picture. The point of this brief detour should be obvious by now. No structure, physical or otherwise, can stand without an invisible and complex infrastructure. This infrastructure gives stability and longevity. In assessing the structure, we need to examine not only its visible parts—in our case the actual claims made about Paul—but also the hidden starting-points, the features that determine its basic shape and texture even before it emerges from the ground—in our case the assumptions and presuppositions of the traditional view. From this it follows that if we seek to dismantle any structure, we need to probe not only its public face but its invisible skeleton as well. Most of these assumptions have already been examined and found to be fragile.

But there are other issues or tendencies involved that are more powerful and less visible. These, too, must be brought to light. They can be summarized as follows:

- Reading back into Paul from later times, importing views developed much later.

- Drawing unjustified universal conclusions from Paul's particular circumstances.

- Reading Paul against ancient Judaism.

Reading Back

There is, of course, no way to read Paul except from the perspective of a later time. Yet there is a difference between the mistaken assumption that his issues were our issues, or even those of his immediate successors, and the historically correct attempt to understand his issues in his time. The difficulty for us is that Paul became, entirely against his own expectations (after all, he foresaw the end of this era in his own lifetime), the central figure in the subsequent history of Christianity and in its Bible, the New Testament. From the first century to the present, he became *the* apostle, the supreme theological authority for every conceivable brand of Christianity, including numerous groups that came eventually to be regarded as heretical. Others, most notably the various Jewish Christian groups that maintained a strong allegiance to Jewish observances, repudiated him as an apostle of Satan. The one issue on which his friends and enemies agreed was that he had rejected the law and Judaism. In other words, Paul's path to his central position in our New Testament was long and tortured. He had to be rescued from his heretical "friends" and "enemies" before he could be restored to the orthodox fold as the canonical spokesman for emergent catholic Christianity. One critic has called the Paul who emerged from this rescue operation "the domesticated apostle."[58]

The central feature of this domesticated Paul, as he appears in the setting of the New Testament, is Christian anti-Judaism. The recurrent message of the Christian communities that created the New Testament between the second and the fourth centuries was the rejection-replacement view of Judaism—Jews had been rejected by God and replaced by a new chosen people, Christians.[59] And the Paul who is installed at the core of the New Testament is taken to be the spokesman, indeed, the originator of that view. From this time on, Christians will read their own anti-Judaism back into Paul. Paul Meyer speaks of it as a "dark Manichaean shadow across the pages of Paul and of his commentators" that has dominated the study of Paul ever since.[60]

The truth of the matter is that the anti-Jewish Paul of the New Testament is not merely "domesticated" but truncated and desiccated—a complete caricature of himself. Nowhere is this more apparent than in the traditional Protestant interpretation of Paul, discussed and dismissed by Krister Stendahl, in which the Reformation's struggle with the Roman Catholic church of the sixteenth century is read back into Paul's supposed debate with Judaism. The result, says Stendahl, is that "Paul's argument has been reversed into saying the opposite to his original intention."[61] Ironically, on issue after issue, later Christianity, for all of its professed loyalty to Paul, failed to adopt his positions on the nature of the resurrection body, on table fellowship between Gentile and law-observant believers[62] and the like. And so, too, I will argue, on the law and Israel.

Generalizing and Universalizing

Closely related to the tendency to read back is the inclination to read Paul as though he were addressing all problems and all times. In a way, this was inevitable, given his role as *the* apostle in the New Testament. Equally inevitable were the consequences—completely de-contextualized and profound misreadings. Quickly, the post-Pauline churches lost sight of the law as an issue within the Jesus-movement and so turned the discussion in Galatians, Romans, and elsewhere into an external, anti-Jewish polemic.

Nowhere has this tendency to universalize been more evident than in the work of Rudolf Bultmann and his students, notably Günther Bornkamm and Ernst Käsemann, who together were the dominant figures in New Testament studies from the 1940s to the 1970s. Despite his own warning not to confuse Paul with Luther (i.e., not to generalize from the particular to the general), Bultmann repeatedly treats Paul as a theologian of the universal human condition.[63] "This willing is the trans-subjective propensity of *human existence as such*."[64] Bornkamm contrasts the letter to the Romans with Paul's other letters:

> Now, in Romans, the ideas and motifs enumerated are not

found, as in the earlier letters, in disconnection and as bearing on this or that actual situation. They are reasoned out,
substantiated more fully and in detail, and given universal
application.[65]

Käsemann, in an essay entitled "Paul and Israel," writes that "the
apostle's real adversary is the devout Jew . . . as the reality of the
religious man."[66] And like his mentor, Bultmann, he denies that
a purely historical reading of Paul is adequate:

> The doctrine [of justification] undoubtedly grew up
> in the course of the anti-Jewish struggle and stands or
> falls with this antithesis. But the historian must not
> make things easy for himself by simply, as historian,
> noting this incontrovertible fact. . . . Our task is to ask:
> what does the Jewish nomism against which Paul fought
> really represent?[67]

The end result is that the specific circumstances of Paul's letters
are lost and, with them, their historical meaning. "Paul's situation as a Jewish 'sectarian' who preached the redemption of the
gentiles became incomprehensible."[68] His law-observant opponents within the Jesus-movement soon became a minority voice.
And the unexpected success of the movement among Gentiles
rapidly pushed it toward becoming a new, separate religion.
Under these conditions, Paul's arguments about the law were no
longer understood as intramural debates within the Jesus-movement but came to be seen as debates between Jews and Christians.
Thus Paul became the theologian of anti-Judaism.

This anti-Jewish Paul has played an enormous role in the
history of Christian dogma and practice. Maurice Goguel put
it well:

> Paul defined the relationship of Christianity with Judaism
> and in this way gave it a structure which was never sub-
> sequently modified . . . and so far as can be seen could never

be called in question without shaking the very foundations of Christianity.[69]

Reading Paul against Judaism

In the late nineteenth and early twentieth centuries, the History-of-Religions school in Germany launched an attack on Jewish portrayals of Paul. Downplaying his self-proclaimed Pharisaic allegiance and emphasizing his origins in the Greek city of Tarsus, adherents of this school drew elaborate parallels between Paul and the so-called pagan mystery-cults (Isis-Serapis, Cybele-Attis, Mithras). Here were the real sources of Paul's piety. No need to examine the vast body of Jewish literature from Paul's lifetime—Philo, Josephus, apocalyptic Judaism (the Dead Sea Scrolls were discovered much later), early Rabbinic literature, and so on. Coupled with an emphasis on his conversion from Judaism, Paul thus emerges as a figure with no Jewish roots. In fact, there appears to be a double isolating effect here: those who stress Paul's break with Judaism, his conversion from Judaism, tend to give little attention to Jewish sources for explaining his thought; and vice versa. At roughly the same time, toward the end of the nineteenth century, a new picture of Greco-Roman Judaism was beginning to emerge among students of early Christianity, a dismal picture whose ignoble origins and pervasive influence have been chronicled by George Foote Moore, Charlotte Klein, and E. P. Sanders.[70] The effect of this unhistorical picture of Judaism, combined with a view of Paul as a convert from Judaism, has been to isolate Paul from Jewish influence, to de-Judaize him.[71]

This de-Judaizing can take the form of locating his roots in "early Hellenistic [i.e., Greek] Christianity" (see Bultmann), a solution that runs parallel to the traditional Jewish argument that Paul's grasp of Judaism had been weakened by his exposure to Greek culture; of stressing the utter novelty of his thinking (Harnack); or of arguing for the impact of Greek "mystery-religions." Of course, there have been discordant voices in the choir. Albert Schweitzer protested vehemently against the History-of-Religions school, insisting that Paul and Hellenism had nothing in common.[72] Instead, Schweitzer looked to apocalyptic Judaism as the soil that nurtured Paul's thought.[73] W. D. Davies, in his *Paul and Rabbinic Judaism. Some Rabbinic Elements in Pauline Theology*, demonstrated extensive parallels between Paul and the later rabbis.[74] But for a variety of reasons, these voices failed to carry the day. Paul remained outside Judaism and scholars were thereby excused from dealing with Paul's Judaism except as "background." As one reader who has sought to re-Judaize Paul has put it, the result of all this is a widely shared premise that "ancient Jewish literature is no source for explaining his letters."[75]

Much the same picture emerges among traditional Jewish readers of Paul, though for very different reasons. If many Christian readers have been eager to protect Paul from Judaism, most Jewish readers have been intent on shielding Judaism from Paul:

- Some argue that he misunderstood or misrepresented Judaism (Buber and Schoeps).

- Others claim that he represented an inauthentic, usually Hellenized form of Judaism (Montefiore, Klausner, and Boyarin).

- Still others, including those most inclined to assert Paul's thoroughgoing Jewishness (Baeck, Rubinstein) point out that he left Judaism behind at some decisive moment (Segal). In any case, his criticisms of Judaism are wide of the mark and his understanding of it unreliable.

But in recent years, as we shall see, a number of readers have come to hold quite different views on these matters. Curiously, or rather, instructively, it is Jewish readers who have emphasized the fundamental discontinuity between the Paul of the letters,

taken in their own time and place, and the anti-Jewish Paul of
the New Testament and later Christianity. Hans Joachim Schoeps
insists that Paul "misunderstood many things" but adds that
"this misunderstanding . . . was repeatedly and far worse misunderstood by his own followers. It may even be asserted . . . that
the whole history of the interpretation of Paul . . . is a single chain
of misunderstandings."[76] And David Flusser remarks that for all
of his influence on later developments, Paul's deep grasp of the
law made little impression.[77]

CHAPTER TWO

NEW VIEWS OF PAUL

*Early in my career as a student of Paul, I was deeply perplexed by his attitude
to the law. To be quite frank about it, I could not understand how a religiously
sensitive Jew such as Paul could speak about the law as he did.*

Michael Wyschogrod

THE ORIGINS OF THE NEW VIEW

Wyschogrod's anguish over Paul is of a piece with the reaction of most Jewish readers and some Christians as well. "The Pauline inference that the law . . . is a law unto death (Rom. 8:2–3; Gal. 3:21) is one which no Jew could draw."[1] "How a Jew of Paul's antecedents could ignore, and by implication deny, the great prophetic doctrine of repentance . . . namely, that God, out of love, freely forgives the penitent sinner and restores him to his favor—that seems from a Jewish point of view inexplicable."[2] And yet it is nothing short of astonishing that until very recently few have been able to anticipate Wyschogrod's simple answer:

The question for Paul is not mainly the significance of Torah for Jews but its significance for Jesus-believing gentiles ... [A]ll the nasty things Paul says about the law are intended to discourage gentiles from embracing the law and are thoroughly misunderstood if they are read as expressions of Paul's opinion about the value of the law for Jews.[3]

In short, Paul did not say nasty things about the law and Israel; he did not draw the inference that the law brought death to Israel; he did not ignore or deny the biblical doctrine of repentance and forgiveness for Israel. This simple insight underlies all recent attempts to rewrite the story of Paul. We can reformulate this insight as a law: *Any statement that begins with the words, "How could a Jew like Paul say X, Y, Z about the law," must be regarded as misguided. In all likelihood Paul, the apostle to the Gentiles, is not speaking about the law as it relates to Israel but only about the law and Gentile members of the Jesus-movement.*

As Lloyd Gaston, one of the major proponents of the new Paul, has put it,

Paul writes to Gentile Christians, dealing with Gentile-Christian problems, foremost among which was the right for Gentiles qua Gentiles, without adopting the Torah of Israel, to full citizenship in the people of God. It is remarkable that in the endless discussion of Paul's understanding of the law, few have asked what a first-century Jew would have thought of the law *as it relates to Gentiles.*[4]

Gentiles turn out to be the pivotal issue in the more far-reaching revisions of the traditional Paul. Indeed, it is not too much to say that there is a direct correlation between these radical revisions and the degree to which the Gentile issue remains the center of attention. To cite one example: those who discuss Paul's conversion without emphasizing, as Paul himself puts it, that "[God] revealed his son to me *so that I should preach him among the*

Gentiles," tend to see the conversion as a movement away from the law and Judaism; contrariwise, those who stress Gentiles as the central theme find continuity.

This phase of the story opened quietly with the work of Krister Stendahl. In the early 1960s, Stendahl delivered a series of lectures, one on "Paul among Jews and Gentiles"[5] and the other "The Apostle Paul and the Introspective Conscience of the West."[6] Today, when many others have finally caught up with Stendahl's initiatives, it is difficult to appreciate just how innovative his original insights were almost forty years ago. In many ways, and with only slight exaggeration, it can be said that subsequent efforts amount to little more than a series of footnotes to his pioneering work. In outline, Stendahl's insights look like this:

- The center of attention is "the apostle to the Gentiles," as Paul describes himself, and his concern for relations between Jews and Gentiles, both within the Jesus-movement and without;[7] any failure to retain this focus can only lead to distortions, misconstructions, and blocked access to Paul's original thought.

- In particular, it was Augustine's "discovery" of Paul's introspective conscience, along with Luther's focus on "justification by faith," that led readers to impose meanings (to read back) that were "absolutely the opposite of what Paul said."[8]

- Modern translations of the Bible regularly reflect this Augustinian and Lutheran Paul.[9]

- In Galatians, Paul is defending his gospel against Judaizers within the Jesus-movement, not against Jews outside.

- In his letter to the Romans, when he does speak about Jews and Israel, Chapters 9–11 represent the culmination of his thinking, not an incidental appendix.

- If Paul argues against anything in Romans it is against the first signs of anti-Semitism among Jesus-worshippers, not against Judaism.[10]

- We should not speak of Paul's conversion as if it implied a transfer out of Judaism; he has no concept of Christianity or of his gospel as a new religion.

- Paul remained a Jew throughout his life; we should always read him within the context of traditional Jewish thought, not against it.

- Paul does not speak of Jews and Judaism in terms of the customary stereotypes put forward by many Christian scholars, (i.e., as "an emasculated prototype of legalism").[11]

- Paul does not conceive of Israel's salvation with reference to Christ; in Romans 10.26, when Paul writes that "All Israel will be saved," he does not say, "Israel will accept Jesus Christ."[12]

Among recent readers of Paul, no one has argued more vigorously for a new view of ancient Judaism than E. P. Sanders. Following on the earlier work of George Foote Moore, W. D. Davies, and others, he has coined the phrase *covenantal nomism* to describe the relationship between redemption and the law in ancient Judaism, that is, the view that

> one's place in God's plan is established on the basis of the
> covenant and that the covenant requires . . . obedience to
> its commandments, while providing means of atonement
> for transgression.[13]

In other words, the covenant with Israel is offered, established, and maintained by God; the law is Israel's response, her part of the bargain. Sanders advances this view in contrast to the persistent Christian conception of Judaism as a religion of works-righteousness, (i.e., the notion that Jews thought of themselves as saved by virtue of their obedience to the law and commandments). We might call Sanders's work the (re-) discovery of ancient Judaism, or rather its rediscovery by non-Jews. For it must be stated that what most Jews have always known, many Christian scholars have learned only lately. As Wyschogrod notes, "It was simply not true that Jews thought they were saved by deeds or works."[14] The lesson to be learned here is that old prejudices die hard.

In a series of widely influential works, Sanders has also brought his work on Judaism to bear on the case of Paul. Having argued that the Judaism of Paul's time offers no evidence to support that traditional picture of Jewish self-righteousness or works-righteousness, he is able to dismiss the notion that Paul's conversion to/by Christ arose from any desire to rise above his Pharisaic self-righteousness. In a line worth repeating, he notes that "the supposed objection [by Paul] to Jewish self-righteousness is as absent from Paul's letters as self-righteousness itself is from Jewish literature."[15] In this respect, he has undermined one of the traditional pillars of Paul-based Christian anti-Judaism.

For all his efforts to undermine the traditional picture of Paul as an insightful critic of ancient Judaism, Sanders nonetheless speaks of "Paul's critique of Judaism."[16] To be sure, Sanders insists that this critique is altogether retrospective, after the fact, and that in some sense the only thing wrong with Judaism for him is that "*it is not Christianity*."[17] Yet at the same time, he can state that

> *Paul in fact explicitly denies that the Jewish covenant can be effective for salvation, thus consciously denying the basis of Judaism.* . . . Paul polemicizes . . . against the prior fundamentals of Judaism: the election, the covenant and the law.[18]

In the end, Sanders remains largely within the old framework and repeats its familiar themes:

- Paul breaks with Judaism, "although he seems not to have perceived that his gospel and his missionary activity imply a break with Judaism."[19]

- Paul denies two fundamental aspects of Judaism—the election of Israel and the need to uphold the law—although Paul himself, as we have seen, specifically maintains that he upholds both.

- Paul moves from Judaism (although he continues to speak of himself as a Jew) to Christianity (although neither he nor anyone else of his generation used the term).[20]

- Paul opposes Jewish particularism, but introduces a particularism of another kind; yet elsewhere it is said "Paul makes the church in theory universal."[21]

- Finally, Sanders reads all of Paul's comments about the law as directed at Israel and the Jews, although at numerous points he also observes that Paul is addressing "his Gentile converts."[22]

Sanders's views are worth dwelling on for a moment, for they typify certain recurrent tendencies among traditional readers. They also illustrate just how difficult it is to dislodge deeply entrenched paradigms. Sanders tends to generalize or universalize Paul's words. Repeatedly he forgets Paul's immediate audience and moves to universal conclusions: for example, "Paul's argument in Rom. 1–4 is *against the necessity of keeping the law*."[23] But for whom? Or, as if the distinction makes no difference, he writes, "Paul himself often formulated his critique of Judaism (or Judaizing)."[24] My contention is that this distinction makes all the difference. For if Paul is addressing and arguing against Jews, then his statements about the law do amount to a fundamental critique of Judaism. On the other hand, if (as Sanders himself frequently recognizes) Paul's immediate audience, at least in Galatians, lies within the Jesus-movement and if his arguments concern the law in relation to his Gentile converts, then his critique has nothing at all to do with Judaism. What is so intriguing about Sanders's work is that he comes so close to a radical break with the traditional view, yet misses it by a mile.

More briefly, we may look at the work of James D. G. Dunn, who regards himself as both a follower and a critic of Sanders. With Sanders and others Dunn argues that Paul had nothing against the law as such or against the idea that the law required good works. "What, then," he asks, "can it be that Paul was objecting to?" What troubled Paul was Judaism's misuse of the law:

- *The law [was] understood and practiced in such a way as to limit the grace of God, in particular, to prevent the Gentiles as gentiles enjoying it in full measure.*[25]

- The law was taken as the basis of "nationalistic zeal,"[26] which manifested itself in "the typically Jewish indictment of Gentile sin"[27] and the "narrower Jewish view which discounts the good done outside the covenant just as it discounts the unrighteousness committed by those within the covenant."[28]

- "Paul objected to the typically Jewish idea that the Gentiles were 'sinners' by definition. . . . To that extent, therefore, we can indeed say that *it was Paul who effectively undermined this third pillar of second Temple Judaism.*"[29]

In some respects, Dunn's work represents a step backward from Sanders. His portrayal of typical Jewish attitudes approaches caricature, as Stowers rightly shows.[30] His emphasis on Jewish ethnic pride reverts to the outmoded, unhistorical dichotomy between Jewish particularism and Christian universalism. Here his position resembles the older view according to which Paul was fully justified in his critique of Judaism. And finally, his treatment of Paul's conversion/commission makes it appear as though the apostle had argued his way out of Judaism, through an internal examination of its shortcomings, whereas Paul himself makes it quite plain that he was transformed, not against or even out of Judaism, but into his calling as the apostle of Christ to the Gentiles.[31]

BASIC ELEMENTS OF THE NEW VIEW

Stendahl's vision of Paul, first laid out in the 1960s, has been slow to gather followers. Even today, when it has gained greater momentum, many readers find themselves unable to accept it, while others follow it only up to a point. The work of Sanders and Dunn demonstrates how difficult it is to break radically with the past.

But for readers like myself, who do accept the new model, it is not a matter of changing a few details. We require a completely new structure. For us, the old model is wrong from top to bottom and its persistence a source of constant amazement. "What is it that casts this dark Manichaean shadow across the pages of Paul and of his commentators?"[32] "It is nonsense to view the Pauline teaching of the Law and justification as an expression of the apostle's anti-Judaism."[33] "The most astonishing presupposition has to do with the major thesis of Romans 9 ... How can people say that Paul teaches the divine rejection of Israel in chapter 9 when he expressly says the opposite (11.1)? ... How has Romans 9 been turned into an anti-Jewish polemic?"[34] "At least since the second century, readers of Paul have come to the texts assuming that God has rejected the Jews ... I believe that Paul assumed just the opposite."[35]

Paul and the Gentiles

There is wide agreement that the Gentiles (*ta ethnē*) stand at the center of Paul's thought and activity. He calls himself the "apostle to the Gentiles" (Rom. 11.13) and "Christ's servant to the Gentiles" (Rom. 15.16); he describes the preaching of the gospel as taking place "among the Gentiles" (Gal. 2.2); when he speaks of his conversion experience, it is in terms of a mission to Gentiles (Gal. 1.16); and in his account of his meeting in Jerusalem with those whom he calls "the leaders" he reports, "they saw that I had been entrusted with the gospel to the Gentiles and gave the right hand of fellowship that we should go among the Gentiles" (Gal. 2.7–9).[36] Nor is there any indication that his own congregations consisted of any but converted Gentiles. Certainly the audience addressed in the letters is always Gentile.

To be sure, the book of Acts paints a somewhat different picture. According to Acts, the apostle regularly proclaims his gospel in local Jewish synagogues.[37] Here we must make a choice: either Acts is fabricating or Paul did preach in synagogues, to Jews, and thereby betrayed his own calling or, as seems much more likely, he did preach in synagogues, but to Gentiles. In fact, we know from numerous sources that Gentiles frequented synagogues throughout the Greco-Roman world. In this case, we may presume that Paul preached to Gentiles in synagogues because he knew that they would already be somewhat attuned to the biblical language and content of his message as he conceived it. Furthermore, this practice would help to explain the hostility exhibited toward Paul, in Acts as well as his own letters, by various Jewish communities, who were surely not happy to see an apocalyptic ex-Pharisee poaching Gentiles from their well-established synagogues.[38]

If this much is clear, it ought to follow that "one would not expect the Apostle to the Gentiles to be engaged in a dialogue with Judaism, but rather with Gentile Christians, explaining how such central concepts as Torah relate to them."[39] Nonetheless, this starting-point, seemingly obvious and straightforward, represents "such a radically new departure"[40] that it has proven difficult for readers to keep their eyes on the target audience. Since the rejection-replacement paradigm is so deeply embedded in our Western culture, it has proven all too easy to slip from knowing that Paul is addressing Gentiles and their relation to the law into assuming that he is contesting the law as it relates to Jews; to move from claiming that the law is no longer incumbent on Gentiles to dismissing it altogether, as irrelevant and outmoded for Jews as well. I cite only one example. At one point Sanders (rightly) observes that in Gal. 3.10 Paul is arguing "to discourage Gentiles from accepting circumcision," but in the next sentence the subject of the sentence changes from the particular, Gentiles, to the universal, one. "In [Gal.] 3.10 Paul argues, citing Deut. 27.26, that one who accepts the law must keep all the laws and that failure to keep them all brings a curse."[41]

This tendency to slip from the particular (Gentiles and the law) to the universal (the law itself and all of humanity, including Jews) when reading Paul illustrates the enormous power of established paradigms. Their resilience resides in the fact that they are hidden, taken for granted, seen as part of the way things are. They are very hard to dislodge, so deeply entrenched are they in our unconscious patterns of perceiving the world. Although many Jewish and Christian readers of Paul have recognized the truth of Gaston's observation (i.e., that Paul is talking to and about Gentiles when he speaks of the law in negative terms), at another level there remains a reluctance or an inability to follow it all the way to its logical conclusion. Thus, in addition to the hesitations of Buber, Segal, Sanders, and Dunn noted earlier, Hans Hübner says the following of the arguments in Galatians:

> We are concerned *no longer with a demonstration of the true character of the religion of the Law but with the unmasking of those* [i.e., within the Jesus-movement] *who are misusing the religion of the Law for their own personal advantage.*[42]

But he continues, as if doubting his own insight:

> However, we would have to ask whether there does not lie concealed behind the inconsistencies of Paul's argument the conviction that the religion of the Law itself is respon-

sible for its representatives sliding imperceptibly into an attitude in which they egotistically misuse the Law.[43]

Here it is hard to avoid the impression that in the first statement Hübner has correctly described the issue (the law and Gentiles in the Jesus-movement), but that somehow the old model (it's really about the law and everyone, i.e., Israel) forces itself onto the scene, in a most peculiar manner, in the second statement.

As a corollary to the centrality of Gentiles in Paul's thought and action, we may add Gaston's claim that the central thrust of Paul's gospel was the inclusion of the Gentiles.[44] Of course, we need to ask, "Inclusion in what?" Various answers have been proposed—Israel, the people of God, the children of Abraham, the righteous, and the promises to Abraham. Some of the possibilities (e.g., the promises to Abraham and his children) seem more appropriate than others (e.g., Israel). Better still would be the redemption or the acceptance of the Gentiles by God.

Paul's Conversion

There is now a broad consensus on issues relating to Paul's conversion/commission:

- Most Jewish and Christian readers agree that Paul's transformation, however we choose to label it, did not involve a movement out of Judaism or from one religion to another; Segal in particular has shown the Jewish character of Paul's language about the experience and its consequences. The only hesitation comes from E. P. Sanders who speaks of Paul as having created a "third entity," but in order to make this claim Sanders is forced to concede that Paul did so "despite himself" and "against his conscious intention."[45]

- Beyond this, there is agreement that the conversion did not come about as a result of any anguish on Paul's part over his inability to fulfill the law or over the law's intrinsic deficiencies; "It was not the inadequacy of Judaism, not the fact that the Judaism which Paul knew was an inferior product . . . that accounts for Paul's conversion, but the impact of the new factor that entered into his ken when he encountered Christ."[46]

- Finally, there is a growing sense not only that Gentiles formed the center of both the conversion experience itself (Gal. 1.16) and its consequences (Paul as apostle to the Gentiles), but that in some sense Gentiles must have been an underlying factor leading up to the conversion. Sanders speculates along the following lines: "If one is to look for secret dissatisfaction . . . it might be better to look to his stance toward the Gentiles than to his possible frustration with his own situation under the law, or to his analysis of the situation of Jews under the law."[47] Gaston considers the possibility that as a zealous Pharisee, whose position was that "there is no hope for the Gentiles except . . . as proselytes," he may have been a missionary among Gentiles even before his commissioning.[48]

Re-Judaizing Paul

If Paul's conversion does not involve a movement out of or against Judaism, it follows that we may begin to relocate him within the religious and social world of Greco-Roman Judaism. On this point, most Jewish and Christian readers are now in full agreement. Some recent Jewish readers have even begun to reclaim Paul, to regard him as "a good Jew, from whom one can learn important things about one's own religion."[49] Among older Jewish readers, Joseph Klausner may be taken as typical: "Paul was a Jew not only in his physical appearance [!], but he was also a typical Jew in his thinking and in his entire inner life."[50] And he continues, "[I]t would be difficult to find more typically Talmudic expositions of Scripture than those in the Epistles of Paul."[51] Some twenty-five years later, H. J. Schoeps could write, "The theology of the apostle arose from overwhelmingly Jewish religious ideas."[52] And in 1993, Daniel Boyarin is prepared to speak of Paul as a "Jewish cultural critic" whose critical challenge must be taken seriously by Jews, "including religious Jews—perhaps especially religious Jews."[53] Elsewhere, in reference to Romans 2, he states that "Paul has essentially produced a sermon to which many if not most Pharisaic preachers could have and would have assented."[54] In some respects, Boyarin is hardly typical of Jewish readers; yet he does represent a relatively new tradition that turns aside from the older attitude, described by Richard Rubinstein in *My Brother Paul* as "Jesus, yes; Paul, never!"[55]

In the end, Boyarin rejects the specific Pauline response to this theological challenge. In so doing he invokes a theme cited frequently by many Jewish and not a few Christian critics of Paul—his Greek, Platonic or Hellenistic mode of thought. Put crudely, the theme opposes "good Judaism" (Pharisaic/Rabbinic, i.e., un- or even anti-Greek and philosophical) to "bad" Judaism (Hellenistic and often seen as embodied in the first-century platonizing philosopher and exegete, Philo of Alexandria). Or, as with Boyarin, Jewish cultural particularism (good) versus Greek and Pauline universalism (bad). There is much wrong with this opposition, quite apart from the question of whether it applies in any way to Paul. Two observations will do for the moment: first, the Pharisees (Paul's group) and the later rabbis belonged to the world of Hellenistic culture just as much as anyone else and Paul is, we need to remind ourselves, the only Pharisee of whom we know anything for certain in the first century; and second, the sort of Judaism represented by Philo and countless others is also Judaism. As historians, we ought not to be in the business of describing one variety as good and all others as bad. Such a choosing of sides looks very much like a retrojection of modern sectarian disputes into a remote and altogether different past.

A brief word about the re-Judaized Paul among Christian readers of Paul. Apart from Albert Schweitzer and W. D. Davies and their thoroughgoing, if one-sided reintegration of Paul into apocalyptic and Rabbinic Judaism, the most important recent developments in producing a new image of Paul have been made possible by relocating the apostle within the broad setting of Greco-Roman Judaism.

In case after case, Lloyd Gaston and Stanley Stowers have loosened knots in the traditional view by showing that a different reading of classic Pauline passages becomes not only possible but necessary when the passages are read in their Jewish context. Consider, for example, the passages in Galatians (and Romans) that speak of the law as a curse and a source of condemnation (e.g., Gal. 3.13: "Christ redeemed us from the curse of the law") Instead of resorting to charges of inconsistency and contradiction in Paul's thought, Gaston observes that in numerous Jewish texts of the time "the concept of Torah had developed in two directions. . . . For Gentiles, who do not have the Torah as covenant, Torah as law functions in an exclusively negative way, to condemn." He cites two examples:[56]

- 4 Ezra 7.20–24 (a Jewish apocalyptic text slightly after Paul's time): "Let many perish who are now living. . . . For God strictly commanded those who came into the world, when they came, what they should do to live. . . . They scorned his law and denied his decrees." And later (7.72): "those who dwell on earth shall be tormented, because though they had understanding they committed iniquity and though they received the commandments they did not keep them."

- Exodus Rabbah 5.9 (a later Rabbinic collection of comments on Exodus): "How did the voice go forth?" Rabbi Tanhuma (fourth century C.E.) said: "The word of the Lord went forth in two aspects, slaying the heathen who would not accept it, but giving life to Israel who accepted the Torah."

These texts by no means represent the full range of Jewish attitudes toward Gentiles in our period. But they do offer a threefold response to one of the major claims of the traditional view: there is no inconsistency here; the double concept of the law (life for some, but death for others) makes sense within Judaism; and the concept restores the audience (Gentile believers) and the issue (Gentiles and the law) of Galatians to their central place in Paul's world. In short, "[t]hose who interpret the passage as an attack on Torah are wrong; it is not the past of Jews which Paul is describing but the past of Gentiles."[57] Here is the solution to the alleged difficulty of "holding together in an integrated whole both the positive and the negative statements regarding the law."[58]

Like Gaston, Stowers repeatedly draws a new portrait of Paul by locating him as a Jew of the first century. In his conclusions, he comments that the de-Judaized traditional Paul "comes out of nowhere." By contrast, the new image makes sense of the apostle "as a complex person fully understandable in the context of the Judaism of his day. . . . This Paul seems plausible as a former Pharisee."[59]

In the end, a re-Judaized Paul leads to a reversal of the law noted earlier: *Christian readers no longer feel compelled to insulate Paul from Judaism, while Jewish readers no longer strive to protect Judaism from Paul.*

The Law Not Rejected for Israel

From each and all of the preceding considerations, it should follow that Paul had no argument against the Jewish law in relation to Israel and the Jews. Yet few have been able to draw this conclusion. Paul Meyer is one of the few to state it plainly: "In fact . . . Paul nowhere suggests that the way to obedience for the Israelite lies in abandoning the Torah."[60] And in his analysis of Paul's use of Jewish law in settling practical matters, Peter Tomson extends the conclusion to Paul himself: "for Paul, as for other Jews, the Law was and remained valid for Jews. . . . [This] was his position in First Corinthians and Galatians; such we may expect it to be in Romans too."[61] Pinchas Lapide, a sensitive Jewish reader of Paul, gets it pretty much right: "For Jews and for

Jewish proselytes the Mosaic law, as Paul sees it, retains its full and unaltered validity."[62]

Wyschogrod's hesitation on this issue in revealing. On the one hand, he correctly sees that Paul's negative comments about the law are "thoroughly misunderstood" if taken as implying anything about its value for Jews.[63] Yet he worries about the statement in Galatians 3.19 to the effect that the law was "added because of transgressions" and "transmitted by angels." "It is difficult to maintain that this is true for gentiles but not for Jews." In similar fashion, David Flusser (with reference to 3.24—"the law was our custodian until Christ came") objects that no Jew could possibly speak of the law as chronologically limited.[64]

Here a basic observation is in order: Wyschogrod's and Flusser's difficulties disappear completely if we apply the law established earlier—*when Paul appears to say something (e.g., about the law and Jews) that is unthinkable from a Jewish perspective, it is probably true that he is not talking about Jews at all. Instead we may assume that the apostle to the Gentiles is talking about the law and Gentiles.*

Early readers of Paul are unanimous in pronouncing that he repudiated the law in principle, that is, for Jews as well as Gentiles. Such a report was in circulation as early as the book of Acts (ca. 120 C.E.): "They have been told about you that you teach all the Jews who are among the gentiles to forsake Moses, telling them not to circumcise their children or to observe the customs." Later Jewish Christians branded Paul as the apostle of Satan and an apostate from the law for similar reasons.[65] And such has been the standard view of Paul from his own time until the present. But, here I find it difficult to disagree with Gaston's assertion that "Paul was completely innocent of the charge . . . and did not encourage Jews to abandon the covenant."[66] What is more, I believe that Paul was painfully aware of this accusation against him and sought to refute it in his letter to the Romans: "Do we overthrow the law through faith? By no means! On the contrary we uphold the law." (3.31) "Is the law sin? By no means!" (7.7) "Has God rejected his people? By no means!" (11.1)

Two Ways?

If Paul's gospel is about the acceptance of the Gentiles and if he does not repudiate the law for Israel, does it follow that Gentiles and Jews take different paths to salvation? Put differently, does Paul foresee the redemption of Israel through conversion to Christ? The traditional answer is typified by W. D. Davies: "At the very limit of history—the Jewish people are forgiven for their culpable hardness, accept Jesus as their Messiah, and thus share in his forgiveness."[67] These are matters of considerable controversy among contemporary readers of Paul.

Paul never speaks of Israel's ultimate redemption as a conversion to Christ. In line with this, an increasing number of readers have spoken of two ways or paths to salvation—through Christ for Gentiles, through the law for Israel. "Paul does not envision Israel's eschatological salvation as its absorption into the Gentile-Christian church . . . Israel has a special eschatological destiny for Paul."[68] "The thesis of the 'special path' by which God at one time will save all Israel appears to the only correct one."[69] "Why will all Israel be saved? . . . It is not said that God will provoke them to faith in Christ, although this is usually assumed without discussion."[70]

Others seem less certain. "[H]e considered that he was *bringing the Gentiles into this Judaism*, and *not taking the Jews out of Judaism* at all. Paul was mistaken in thinking this."[71] "Paul . . . does not draw a detailed picture of what he envisions at the end of time, when some of Israel will embrace Christianity. . . . Paul implies that only those who accept Christ will be saved . . . but, strangely, he does not actually state it. . . . Paul does not state exactly how the process of redemption for Jews will come about."[72]

Stowers's position on the idea of two ways is certainly the most nuanced. His answer is Yes and No. On the Yes-side, he repeatedly emphasizes Paul's separate treatment, even at the level of ordinary language, of Jews and Gentiles. "Israel does have a relation to Christ's faithfulness, although Paul speaks as if it differs from that of gentiles. . . . The whole discussion of Rom. 9–11 has its premise in the assumption of separate but interrelated end-time destinies for Jews and gentiles."[73] On the No-side, he holds, against Gaston, that Paul did understand Jesus Christ to be Israel's future messiah.[74] He cites Romans 1.16 ("The gospel . . . is the power for salvation, for the Jew first and then the Greek") as indicating some role for Christ in the redemption of Israel.[75] But even in this case, Stowers makes important modifications in the traditional view: first, Paul's messianic language is described as "mostly alien to those [Jewish] messianic traditions," which would appear to bring him close to Gaston's view that Paul's Jesus is not the Messiah understood primarily as "the climax of God's dealing with Israel;"[76] and second, the meaning of Romans 1.16 becomes clear only later in 15.5–13, when Christ's ministry is presented as confirming God's promises to redeem Gentiles![77] Thus Stowers summarizes the classic passage of Romans 10.4 ("Christ is the goal [*telos*] of the law with respect to righteousness for all who believe") as "Christ is the goal of the law with respect to God's plan to redeem the gentiles."[78]

One final observation on the "two ways." It would be a serious misrepresentation of Paul's to say that he conceived of separate or divided paths as the final word. In the one passage (1 Corinthians 15.24–28) from his writings in which he imagines the ultimate state of the cosmos, he speaks in theo-logical, that is, mono-theistic, rather than christo-logical language:

> Then comes the end when he [Christ] delivers the kingdom to God after destroying every ruler. . . . When all things are subjected to him, then the Son himself will also be subjected to him [i.e., to God] who put all things under him, so that God may be everything to everyone (or: all in all).

In this eschatological scenario, even Christ is subordinated in a way that finally reveals Paul as a thoroughly Jewish monotheist.

In other respects, too, it is clear that Paul thinks of the two ways as a temporary, provisional stage in the story of salvation.

- Abraham is the father of both Jews and Gentiles; they are one seed, one inheritance.

- Abraham's faith/faithfulness is source and model for Jews and Gentiles.

- The promise to Abraham (Rom. 4.13), that is, to be the father of many Gentiles (Gen. 17.5; quoted in Rom. 4.17), is one.

In the end, there are not two peoples of God but one. Jews and Gentiles—humanity in its entirety—form one corporate body, not identical with Israel and certainly not with any Christian church. They are seen as common heirs ("the Jew first and then the Greek"— Rom. 1.16; 2.10) of the divine promise to Abraham, as the children of God (Rom. 8.19).

Gentiles and the End of History

These references to the end of time and the ultimate state of the cosmos introduce a new theme, one that lies at the very center of Paul's life and work. For in addition to his mission as the apostle to the Gentiles, the other fundamental consequence of his conversion was a conviction that he was living in the final days of history: "I consider that the sufferings of the present time are not worth comparing with the glory that is to be revealed to us." (Rom. 8.18); "The trumpet will sound, the dead will be raised and we shall be changed." (1 Cor. 15.52); "For salvation is nearer to us than when we first believed; the night is far gone, the day is at hand" (Rom. 13.11f.).

Of course Paul was not alone in his conviction that the end was near. He shared this with virtually every strand of the early Jesus-movement (the gospel of John and its community seems to be an exception) and with many other Jews of his time. To ignore this all-consuming orientation, or to downplay it, is to misread Paul at every turn. However inconvenient it may be for modern readers who seek to appropriate Paul as a solution to modern problems, this intense eschatological mentality underlies his every thought and action.

In particular, it is now clear that Paul's preoccupation with the Gentiles remains incomprehensible apart from his eschatological framework. For it had long been a central belief in many streams of Judaism that in the final stage of history God would incorporate or redeem righteous Gentiles into the people of God. Leo Baeck put it succinctly: "The 'coming' of the Messiah and the 'coming' of the gentiles are interconnected. This is Jewish faith and such was Paul's faith."[79] For some this meant conversion to Judaism and acceptance of full Torah observance.[80] For others, the Gentiles' path to salvation "on that day" led not through conversion and circumcision but to redemption "*as Gentiles*, rather than as converts to Judaism."[81] This point is worth emphasizing: there were Jewish precedents for Paul's notion that the salvation of the Gentiles or their attainment of righteousness did not require conversion to Judaism and, for males, circumcision.

These two divergent paths for Gentiles—the one through conversion and circumcision, the other not—reappear violently within the Jesus-movement, both in its earliest stages and later in the struggles between mainstream Christianity and the various forms of Jewish Christianity. Early on, within the Jesus-movement, heated disputes arose over the status of Gentile believers. Were they first to be made Jews, and for men, to undergo circumcision (so James the brother of Jesus; Peter; Paul's apostolic opponents in Galatians and Philippians; and the "men from Judea" in Acts 15.1 who preached, "Unless you are circumcised according to the custom of Moses you cannot be saved")? Or were they saved as Gentiles, via a path different from that of Israel (so Paul)? Thus the issues within the Jesus-movement were identical with those under debate among Jews at large—the conditions for the salvation of Gentiles and the practice of circumcision. Paul clearly falls into one of these traditions and not the other.

A few brief comments will clarify this important element in the new picture of Paul. First, the practice of actual Jewish communities in the Greco-Roman world lends support to the notion that not all Gentiles were required to be circumcised in order to participate in the life of synagogues. An important inscription from the city of Aphrodisias (Asia Minor, present-day Turkey) cites an organization within the local Jewish community ("the committee of ten, [called] students of the law and those who fervently praise God"), which included among its members Jews, proselytes (full Gentile converts), and God-fearers (*theosebeis*).[82] To be sure, the inscription dates from a later period (third century C.E.), but I see no reason to doubt that it represents a long-established practice.

Second, and closer to Paul's time, are two much debated texts from the first century C.E.—one from Philo of Alexandria, Paul's contemporary, and the other from Josephus, who was slightly younger. Both texts clearly indicate that the circumcision of Gentiles was a topic of discussion among Jews of the time. Philo, citing Exodus 22.21 ("You shall not oppress the sojourner/stranger [*prosêlutos*] for you were strangers in Egypt"), comments as follows: "Scripture makes it clearly apparent . . . that the sojourner is one who circumcises not his uncircumcision but his desires and sensual pleasures."[83] Josephus relates the story of certain Izates, king of Adiabene, who embraced Judaism but was persuaded by his mother to avoid circumcision lest it offend his subjects. Izates's Jewish mentor, a merchant named Ananias, agreed with the advice and instructed Izates as follows:

> The king could worship God even without being circumcised
> if indeed he had fully decided to be a devoted adherent of
> the Jewish traditions, for it was this that mattered more
> than circumcision.[84]

Neither of these texts argues against circumcision for Jews or for full converts. Nor does Paul. But they do establish a point made by Paul (Rom. 2.13—"For it is not hearers of the law but does of the law who will be justified") and numerous other Biblical and Jewish texts, namely, that "true circumcision was a matter of the heart without ever supposing an elimination of physical circumcision."[85] Except, in Paul's case, for Gentiles at the end of days.

Israel and the End of History

Paul's elaborate scenario for the end of time, which he presents as a divine mystery (i.e., revelation), is laid out in Romans 9–11:

- Israel has stumbled/trespassed/been hardened so that God can redeem the Gentiles.

- When Israel sees what God has done and becomes jealous, "All Israel will be saved."

- Gentiles have no cause to boast, for they have been grafted as wild shoots onto the cultivated olive tree and can just as easily be cut off; the issue in Romans 9-11 is Gentile boasting, not Jewish.

- All of this is revealed, laid out and predicted in scripture.

- All of this is to transpire in the near future, certainly in Paul's lifetime.

There is no real disagreement among old and new readers on these basic "facts." What is new, in the work of Gaston, Stowers, and others, flows from and reinforces all of the preceding elements in the new portrait of the apostle. There are four main issues, laid out similarly by Gaston and Stowers:

1. There is no hint anywhere that God has rejected Israel, although Paul had reason to believe that some of his readers might draw this false conclusion (11.1—"Has God rejected his people? By no means!"). Thus there is no contradiction between Chapters 9 and 10, commonly thought to be harshly critical

of Israel, and Chapter 11, where he is often accused of inconsistency in that he is unable to follow his criticisms to their logical conclusion, that is, the final rejection of Israel. The issue is still God's election of Israel and the futility of Gentile boasting; the criticism is directed not at Israel but at the church.[86] Stowers shows that Paul lays a rhetorical trap for his Gentile audience in his use of remnant language in 9.6 ("For not all who are descended from Israel belong to Israel and not all are children of Abraham because they are his descendants"); in line with biblical and later Jewish texts, Paul uses the remnant motif not to replace Israel with some new entity but to demonstrate "God's way of guaranteeing that Israel will be preserved."[87]

2. While Israel has momentarily stumbled (Rom. 9.32), failed to achieve righteousness (9.30), and been hardened (11.7), none of this is the result of Israel's own doing; as with Pharaoh (9.17; 11.8–10), God has hardened Israel for his own purposes, that is, to demonstrate that he shows mercy on whomever he chooses, in this case the Gentiles. That Israel's present status (failing to obtain what it sought—Rom. 11.7) is none of its own doing is further reinforced by the metaphor of the "fixed" footrace that runs throughout Chapters 9–11; the race is fixed in that its outcome depends not on any human effort but solely on God's mercy (9.16). Because God placed a stumbling stone in Israel's path and because, in Paul's thinking, Israel's failure was a necessary part of God's scheme to redeem the Gentiles. In short, Israel never had a chance.

3. While it is theoretically possible that Paul could have imagined a different outcome, that is, Israel would have understood that God's righteousness meant the redemption of the Gentiles through Christ, God had chosen to pursue a different course. Why this had to be Paul never fully explains. He struggles with these issues in 9.14–26, asking "Is there injustice on God's part?" His rhetorical answer is that God can do whatever he wants

(9.19: "Who are you, a mere human, to quarrel with God?").
His scriptural solution is to juxtapose passages that speak of
God's righteous wrath with texts from Exodus (Pharaoh) and
the prophet Hosea that speak of God's plan to redeem those
outside of Israel (9.25, citing Hosea 2.23: "Those who were not
my people I will call my people and her who was not my
beloved I will call my beloved"). In other words, he insists, God
has always used his anger with Israel as a means of bringing
redemption to the Gentiles.

4. One final word: Paul's rhetorical and scriptural arguments to
   the contrary, there are no real precedents in ancient Judaism
   or the Hebrew Bible for the totality of this end-time scenario.
   It is entirely the product of Paul's fertile imagination.

BASIC PRESUPPOSITIONS OF THE NEW VIEW

Presuppositions or assumptions are forces that move interpretations in one direction or another. Some of them are conscious and deliberate; most are hidden and thus unexamined. These
latter are not seen as assumptions at all, but are taken to be just
the way things are. There is no such thing as an interpretation
without presuppositions. They do more than shape interpretations; they make them. Bad presuppositions produce bad readings. New ones yield new readings. Unexamined presuppositions
generally reinforce old readings.

Settings as the Key

Paul was not writing to the church of Augustine in the fourth
century, or to the Protestant Reformers of the sixteenth century, or to post-Holocaust Christians in the twentieth century. This
sounds silly. Yet this is precisely how the apostle to the Gentiles
has been read throughout Christian history. To be more precise,

since official Christianity has persistently defined itself against Judaism, Christian readers have assumed that the great apostle must also have been writing against Judaism. Scholarly readers—those who seek to determine what Paul said and meant in his time—know that this is not so, but even they have great difficulty in defining the settings of his letters and in keeping their gaze fixed on them. Their eyes wander. When they do, they come to rest on old settings, old assumptions. In short, understanding the settings in which Paul worked, taught, and wrote his letters is decisive in determining their meaning in their time. What were they?

The first setting locates Jews and Judaism among Gentiles before the first century. Judaism was a major religious and social force in the Greco-Roman world; Diaspora Jewish communities had existed in most cities for more than 300 years before Paul began to preach his gospel. Although there are occasional signs of anti-Jewish sentiments among the disaffected literati of Rome and Alexandria (Egypt), many non-Jews found the synagogues of the Jews to be open, welcoming, and attractive; Josephus, the first century Jewish historian gives an accurate account of this state of affairs—"the masses have long since shown a keen desire to adopt our religious observances; and there is not one city, Greek or barbarian, nor a single nation, to which our custom of abstaining from work on the seventh day has not spread ... as God permeates the universe, so the Law has found its way among all humanity."[88] As for the attitude of synagogues toward these Gentile adherents, Josephus notes that "he [Moses] gives a gracious welcome, holding that it is not family ties alone which constitute relationship but agreement in the principles of conduct."[89]

Thus, when Paul took his gospel of Christ and the salvation of the Gentiles into the cities of the Greco-Roman world, he encountered not only well-established Jewish communities but significant numbers of Gentiles associated with them. Some became full converts (proselytes), while others occupied an intermediate status as God-fearers. The book of Acts portrays Paul's preaching activity as taking place primarily in such communities (13.4–14, 14–52; 14.1–7, 8–20; 16.11–40; 17.1–9, 10–15, 16–34; 18. 1–17, 18–23; 19.1–41; 28.16–31). By failing to understand the broad setting of Judaism in the Greco-Roman world, many have misread these passages and assumed that the apostle to the Gentiles really did preach to and against Jews after all. I believe that on this issue the author of Acts was probably right—Paul did preach in synagogues, but to Gentiles! Acts is also right on a second motif in these accounts, namely, that Paul's activities generated deep hostilities toward him among many Jews. These hostilities are reflected directly in two Pauline texts: first, in 2 Corinthians 11, where he speaks of "danger from my own people" and of having received thirty-nine lashes (an official punishment administered by Jews on Jews[90]) five times at the hands of the Jews, no doubt in connection with his disruptive missionary activities; and second, in 1 Thessalonians 2, an early letter, where he rants against the Jews "who killed both the Lord Jesus and the prophets and drove us out and . . . oppose all men by hindering us from speaking to the Gentiles that they may be saved." If this passage is authentically Pauline, the phrase "hindering us from speaking to Gentiles" merely confirms the picture painted in Acts.[91]

In short, efforts to spread the message of Jesus Christ among Gentiles encountered both competition and resistance from Jewish communities. One of the standard Christian responses to this resistance was the claim that it was Christians, not Jews, who were the True Israel; indeed, that Christians had replaced Jews as the People of God. What is more, Christians regularly made this claim in Paul's name. The book of Acts puts this message into Paul's mouth at every turn,[92] and the Latin-writing theologian of the late second century C.E. "knew" that "the primary epistle against Judaism is that addressed to the Galatians."[93] This is the setting in which Paul's letters have been read from that day till this. But it was not the setting in which he wrote the letters and the message is not his.

The second setting concerns the early Jesus-movement itself.

In contrast to the harmonious tale told by the author of Acts, it is clear that the early decades of the movement's development witnessed deep divisions over the Gentile question: Were Gentiles admissible at all? If so, under what conditions? Did they need to convert to Judaism and, for males, undergo circumcision? Or were they to be accepted as Gentiles? Could Torah-observant believers associate and/or eat with nonobservant followers? These questions racked the movement from the very beginning and remained alive for at least 600 years thereafter.

The Torah-observant stream, those whom Acts calls Hebrews (6.1) and the circumcision-believers (10.45)—including the "false brethren" whom Paul associates with Jerusalem; James, the brother of Jesus; Peter and his own co-worker Barnabas (Gal. 2); and many nameless others—not only insisted on circumcision for Gentile believers but actively and persistently combated Paul and his gospel. We need not think of this opposition as a single, unified party but rather as a broad stream within the Jesus-movement as a whole. What is clear is that groups representing this view hounded Paul's efforts, followed him from place to place, preaching against his gospel and winning over many members of his congregations to their point of view, that is, that circumcision was necessary for Gentile followers of Jesus.

Unmistakable evidence of these anti-Pauline apostles, within the Jesus-movement, appears in Galatians, Philippians, and 2 Corinthians. These are the enemies at whom he directs his anger and his arguments. This is the setting for his statements about the law and circumcision—disputes within the Jesus-movement, not with Jews or Judaism outside.

Early Misunderstandings of Paul's Gospel

As early as the book of Acts (ca. 100 C.E.), Paul was understood to be the teacher of the rejection-replacement view of Judaism. At roughly the same time, another author (2 Peter) writes of "false teachers" who had twisted Paul's difficult teachings, though with no mention of circumcision and the Gentiles. In other words, he had become the focus of major disputes within the circles of emergent Christianity toward the end of the first century. But it now seems clear to me that such misreadings had already arisen within Paul's lifetime, that he was fully aware of them, and that his letters were intended to counter and correct them. This has long been accepted as true for other issues (e.g., his position on sex and marriage in 1 Corinthians), but has not been fully exploited for what appears to have been the heart of his gospel, the new status of Gentiles.

Paul himself points in this direction. Others have been slow to follow. In Romans 3.8, in the midst of a discussion on Jews and Gentiles and immediately following his voluble retort that circumcision is of value (for Jews) in every way (3.2), he protests, "Why am I still being condemned as a sinner . . . Their condemnation is justified." In short, one of the apostle's chief concerns in his letter to the Romans is to correct certain misreadings of his gospel. "In Romans . . . one of the purposes is to refute false rumors that Paul had rejected the Law and his own people."[94] "Paul, for his part, is laboring to refute the charge—whether rhetorical or historical—that *he*, as a promulgator of a startling new teaching incorporating uncircumcised Gentiles into the people of God, has abandoned the ways of the God of Israel."[95] But who were these critics? Possibly Jews outside the movement. Much more likely, however, they were not critics at all, but rather "followers" of Paul, like the author of Acts, who were speaking in his name. "Paul's questions are not merely rhetorical and . . . the objector is not necessarily Jewish."[96] The real enemy stalked within.

Paul and Rhetoric

In the end, Paul's efforts were unsuccessful. Why was this so? A partial answer to our question lies in Paul's use of rhetoric. One of the most important (re-) discoveries in recent years has been the rhetorical character of Paul's letters. Notable among these have been Rudolf Bultmann, in his early work on elements borrowed from the Cynic-Stoic diatribe/sermon;[97] the classicist, Arnaldo Momigliano in a brief note;[98] and the historian of ancient rhetoric, George Kennedy, in a lengthy study of rhetoric in the New Testament.[99] In the recent work of Hans Dieter Betz (on Galatians) and Stanley Stowers,[100] Neil Elliott,[101] and John Lodge (on Romans 9–11),[102] rhetorical analysis has moved beyond purely formal observations (e.g., that Paul used this or that feature of Greco-Roman rhetorical) to matters of substance. Stowers states the case in its strongest terms: "I am convinced that the way one construes audience and author in the rhetoric of the letter is the decisive factor in determining the reading one will give to the letter [Romans]."[103] Recent discussion has focused on two areas:

1. The use of *prosôpopoiia*, that is, character sketches or impersonations within the text that represent the voice and the views of persons other than and often quite different from those of the author (Stowers calls this speech-in-character); and

2. The use of the incompetent or unreliable author, as a rhetorical strategy, especially in the letter to the Romans.

Prosôpopoiia

Quintilian, the great Roman professor of rhetoric, a slightly younger contemporary of Paul, describes this figure of speech:

> With this figure we present the inner thoughts of our adversaries as though they were talking with themselves . . . . Or without diminishing our credibility we may introduce conversations between ourselves and others, or of others among themselves and give words of advice, reproof, complaint, praise, pity to appropriate persons.

Quintilian calls this technique impersonation (*fictiones person-arum*) and uses the Greek term *prosôpopoiia*. Ancient readers, schooled in rhetoric, would have been alert to such changes in voice within a text or speech. Modern readers, unfamiliar with these techniques, tend to give a flat, tone-deaf reading, assuming that one single voice is at work throughout. We tend to assume that all the views, like all the words, must be Paul's.

Stowers, building on the insights of ancient Christian commentators, insists that Paul deploys the technique of speech-in-character [i.e., impersonation] throughout his letter to the Romans (e.g., 2.1–16, 17–29; 3.1–9; 3.27–4.2 and Chapter 7).[104] Two brief examples will suffice:

1. In Romans 7 the author speaks of "his" inability to fulfill the law, overcome by the greater power of sin. For centuries this text has served as the cornerstone of the notion that for Paul the law was weak, ineffective, and destined for elimination by Jesus Christ. In 1929, W. G. Kümmel argued that the text could not be read as autobiographical in any manner.[105] What he did not realize was that his conclusions had been anticipated much earlier, precisely on rhetorical grounds, by ancient Christian commentators—Origen, Rufinus, and Jerome.[106] Nilus of Ancyra (a Christian writer of the fifth century) observed that Paul is not speaking of himself. Nilus comments, "It is easy to grasp that the apostle is employing characterization (*ēthopoiia*) when a voice says "But I was living without the law." . . . Moreover the person is to be understood as belonging to those who have lived outside the law of Moses [i.e., Gentiles]."[107]

2. Romans 2.17–29 has provided another pillar for the structure of Paul's alleged rejection of the law and Judaism. Paul addresses a fictive character as follows: "But if you call yourself a Jew and rely upon the law and boast of your relation to God . . . you who teach others will you not teach yourself? While you preach against stealing, do you steal?" Bultmann treats this as

a characteristic example of human and especially Jewish boast-ing,[108] while Käsemann labels it as "a concrete attack on the Jews."[109] But Stowers is able to show, using examples from rhetor-ical sources, that the figure of the Jew addressed by Paul rep-resents a standard type, "the pretentious teacher," one who is a philosopher in name only. Epictetus, another younger con-temporary of Paul, is fond of poking fun at those who are Stoics in name alone; "Why did you pride yourself on things that were not your own? Why did you call yourself a Stoic?"[110] Furthermore, in another lecture on the same topic, he repeats the question, "Why do you call yourself a Stoic?" and then immediately quotes what must have been a widely known aphorism: "He is not real-ly a Jew, he is only acting the part."[111] In other words, far from being an attack on Judaism or the law, Romans 2.17–29 puts forward a well-known fictive character—the Jew in name only—as a means of justifying Paul's role as the true teacher of the Gentiles.

The Unreliable Author

Paul regularly employs a deliberate method of argumentation that has been little recognized. Throughout the letter to the Romans, but also in Galatians, he pursues a line of reasoning that seems straightforward, only to assault his readers with their utter mis-understanding. "What then is the advantage of the Jew? And what is the value of circumcision." (3.1); "Should we continue in sin so that grace may abound?" (6.1; cf. 6.15); "Is there injustice on God's part?" (9.14); "I ask then, Has God rejected his people?" (11.1); "Have they [Israel] stumbled so as to fall?" (11.11); "Is the law against the promises of God?" (Gal. 3.21). The questions anticipate, even encourage, one answer but in the end demand another.

In each case, Paul's strategy is to mislead his readers into assum-ing that his conclusions are identical with theirs; but at the moment of climax he reveals that they are the very opposite. He plays the role of what John Lodge calls the unreliable author: "[T]he naïve acceptance of all the viewpoints of the implied author leads to a misunderstanding." "The argument in chaps. 9 and 10 deliberately refrained from revealing Paul's assumption all along that Israel's 'stumble' is not so as to fall." "[A]n unreliable implied author continues to tempt anti-Israel implied readers."[112] In similar fashion, the literary critic Wayne Booth describes the "deliberately deceptive" author as one who must "deceive in order to trap his auditors and readers into judging him first so that he can then turn the judgment back upon them."[113]

But this is a risky business, for readers can easily miss the point. At worst, they will construct a Paul who really did believe that Israel's "stumble" was hard and permanent. At best, they will accuse him of contradiction and inconsistency.

A FINAL NOTE—HOW CAN THIS BE?

A skeptical reader might well ask at this point, "How can you claim that two thousand years of readers have misread Paul? Not just on matters of detail, but even to the point of completely reversing his view of the law and Israel!" Not an unreasonable question. In fact, anyone making such a claim must shoulder an enormous burden of proof. I take this to mean not just that I may advance a new way to read Paul but that at the same time I must offer an account of how the misreading came to be in the first place and why it persisted so long.

Proponents of the "new" Paul have not been unaware of this burden. "Why letters specifically addressed to Gentiles should have been understood as opposing Judaism is not hard to explain."[114] The "loss of Paul's historical and cultural context and the concerns of later Christianity led to a different Paul."[115] More pointedly, W. D. Davies notes that "when his letters came to be read by Gentiles who little understood Judaism, the misinterpretation became almost inevitable."[116]

My only quibble with Davies is that his "almost" seems

unnecessary. When we lose sight of the immediate settings of Paul's letters and assume—with all subsequent readers—that his audience and opponents were Jews rather than anti-Pauline apostles within the Jesus-movement. When we read Paul through the lens of the book of Acts and the New Testament canon. When we read back into Paul the rejection-replacement and triumphalist theology of early (and later) Christianity. When we ignore the intense eschatological framework of Paul's thought and action. When we read Paul with no eye or ear for his rhetorical strategies. When we come to Paul with a preconceived notion of Judaism that is an unrecognizable parody of historical reality. When we discard efforts to invent a "new" Paul because of their "fateful significance for the whole of Christianity."[117] In short, when we read Paul within alien frameworks, the old view becomes not just explicable but inevitable.

CHAPTER THREE

THE LETTER TO THE GALATIANS

*Paul developed his teaching about the law and justification not against
Jews, but against fellow Christians! For the most part this is ignored by
Christian interpreters of Galatians, even though this observation provides the
hermeneutical key to understanding the letter.*

Franz Mussner

Galatians typifies the circumstances under which Paul wrote all of his surviving letters. In modern terms, we would call them attempts at damage control. The newly commissioned apostle to the Gentiles traveled throughout the northeastern rim of the Mediterranean basin, preaching his gospel of Christ. According to the book of Acts, he sometimes addressed himself to Gentiles in synagogues; at other times he must have found other venues, public and private, for conveying his message. I believe that there are solid grounds for assuming that many of Paul's converts, including those in Galatia, were Gentiles with prior connections to synagogues. In any case, we know that he would spend a period of time wherever he met with success, teaching and helping the newly founded church to establish itself. These churches were very much Paul's congregations, brought into being by "his" gospel. They must have been quite small. And they consisted entirely of Gentiles. When Paul writes to these congregations, he always addresses them as Gentiles.

When Paul moved on, seeking new converts and building new communities, he did not lose contact with his other churches. Occasionally he would retrace his steps to visit them in person. In addition, co-workers moved back and forth between Paul and his network of churches, carrying messages and letters (e.g., Timothy in 1 Thessalonians 3.1–6; Epaphroditus, "my co-worker," in Philippians 2.25; anonymous figures in 2 Corinthians 9.3).

For the most part, his surviving letters deal with problems and crises that came to Paul's attention through these communications. 1 Corinthians refers to "the matters about which you wrote" (7.1); and in Philippians and Galatians, addressed to widely separated regions, Paul deals with reports concerning anti-Pauline apostles who were challenging his authority and insisting that his Gentile (male) converts needed to undergo circumcision in order to be saved: "Some [Jesus-followers] came down from Judea and were teaching the followers, 'Unless you are circumcised according to the custom of Moses, you cannot be saved'"(Acts 15.1). Paul's gospel, by contrast, held that Gentiles had been redeemed by Christ and that for them the law was no longer relevant; indeed, Gentiles had lain under a curse before Christ and had now been released from that curse.

These issues generated deep and bitter divisions within the early Jesus-movement. Even the book of Acts, notorious for its efforts to smooth over difficulties, confesses that "Paul and Barnabas had no small dissension with them ['the men from Judea']." Both sides were unrelenting and active in combating their antagonists. In Paul's case, we know that his opponents followed him from place to place, seeking to undo the "damage" he had done (Acts 15.1: "Unless you are circumcised according to the custom of Moses, you cannot be saved"). Paul fought back. In Philippians he warns his converts, "Look out for the dogs, look out for the evil-doers, look out for those who mutilate the flesh" (3.2–3).

In Galatians, a similar crisis had arisen. In a word, anti-Pauline apostles *within the Jesus-movement* had persuaded members— some? most? all? Paul does not say—of his congregation to accept circumcision and to follow at least some elements of the Mosaic law. The apostle is angry and offended (1.6: "I am astonished that you are so quickly deserting him who called you . . . and turning to another gospel" and 3.1: "You stupid Galatians! Who has bewitched you?"). Who these teachers were is not clear. Were they Gentiles, like the Galatians themselves, who were convinced that the path to redemption for all, Jew and Gentile alike, led through Israel? Or were they Jewish followers of Jesus, like those whom the book of Acts calls the "circumcision party" and "believers from the Pharisees?" Judging by the narrative in 2.1–14, Paul seems to connect them to the "false brethren," the "men from James [the brother of Jesus]," and even to Peter, all of whom resisted his law-free gospel to the Gentiles.

As for the content of the "different gospel," circumcision was the key issue. Only those who belonged to the people of Israel were deemed justified or saved.[1] Along with circumcision (Hebrew *berith*), which symbolized membership in the covenant community of Israel, there may have been a limited observance of other elements from the Mosaic law/covenant (Hebrew *berith*). The most likely scenario is that both the "troublemakers" and their followers had adopted some form of selective observance. This much seems to be implied in Paul's sarcastic aside that "even those who receive circumcision do not themselves keep the law" (6.13). In the same vein, his counterargument that "everyone who receives circumcision is bound to keep the whole law" (5.3) makes sense only if full observance was not the case. What this selective observance entailed is not clearly indicated. 4.10 states, "You observe days, months, seasons and years." Whether this indicates religious observances already undertaken, or merely under consideration, as Betz contends; whether the observances are thought to be Jewish or pagan; and whether it is merely a typically unflattering portrait of "superstitious" behavior, the point is that what the Galatians are doing is the very opposite of what Paul intended. And, as he argues, it has placed them in great danger for, as he argues throughout, the law had always meant condemnation for Gentiles.

THE AUDIENCE

The letter addresses these circumstances. The issue is the law as it relates to Gentiles. His audience is a Gentile congregation. His opponents are missionaries within the Jesus-movement. In Gaston's words, "One would not expect the Apostle to the Gentiles to be engaged in a dialogue with Judaism, but rather with Gentile Christians, explaining how such central concepts as Torah relate to them."[2]

To keep this premise in mind is to find the key to reading the letter in a new way. To lose sight of it is to read the letter in the old-fashioned way, as directed at Judaism, and to recreate the old Paul. How hard it is to keep ones eyes on the target and how easy to slip into old ways is a discouraging cautionary tale for all readers!

The literary character of the letter deserves some mention. Only recently has its rhetorical structure come to be fully appreciated. It is not a hastily composed note but an artfully crafted epistle, reflecting and modifying the norms of Greco-Roman rhetoric. H. D. Betz assigns it to the category of the apologetic letter, in which an author presents a self-defense/apology to an audience.[3] Such letters generally combine "reflections on eternal problems and personal experiences."[4] Additionally, Betz uses the category of magical letter to describe Galatians.[5] In other words, Paul does not rely on persuasive arguments alone but invokes higher powers to curse his opponents (1.8–9: "Let him be accursed . . . let him be accursed") and to bless his loyal followers (6.16: "Peace and mercy be on all who walk by this rule"). He is even prepared to believe that the Galatians themselves have been led astray by spells (3.1: "Who has bewitched [*ebaskanen*] you?").

In a slightly different vein, George Kennedy has argued that we should instead treat Galatians as an example of judicial or deliberative rhetoric.[6] Several aspects of the Roman rhetor Quintilian's treatment of deliberative rhetoric are directly pertinent to our reading of Galatians:

1. "Sometimes definition is necessary . . . this is especially the case where there is some doubt of the legality of the course under discussion" (3.8.4); of course, legal matters and language lie at the very heart of Galatians.

2. "The deliberative department of oratory (also called advisory), while it deliberates about the future, also inquires about the past, while its functions are twofold and consist in advising and dissuading" (3.8.6); the letter dwells on the past and the future; persuading and dissuading define Paul's purpose in writing.

3. In the opening *exordium*, whose purpose is to win the favor of the audience, "we may begin with a reference to ourselves or to our opponent" (3.8.6–9); Paul begins by presenting both himself and his opponents.

4. Speaking of the "statement of facts" and the presentation of "external matters," Quintilian states that these elements are optional when everyone is "well acquainted with the issue" (3.8.10); obviously Paul felt the need to (re-)acquaint his readers with the facts, which led him to the extended account of his past encounters with Peter and the Jerusalem leaders (1.11–2.21).

5. "Anger has frequently to be excited or assuaged and the minds of the audience have to be swayed to fear, ambition, hatred, reconciliation . . . the orator may . . . indulge his passion to

some extent" (3.8.12f); expressions of anger run throughout the letter as Paul seeks to reconcile his converts to his gospel.

6. "But what really carries the greatest weight in deliberative speeches is the authority of the speaker. For he ... should both possess and be regarded as possessing genuine wisdom and excellence of character" (3.8.12f.); Paul's authority (from God as well as from the leaders in Jerusalem) is the central issue in the letter; his concluding personal remarks make the point unmistakably (6.11—"See with what large letters I am writing to you with my own hand" [i.e., Paul's signature embodies his authoritative presence] and 6.17—"Henceforth let no one trouble me; for I bear on my body the marks of Jesus").

THE ISSUES AND ARGUMENTS.

I have no intention of writing a commentary on Galatians. Instead, following Mussner's and Gaston's example and focusing on passages that have traditionally been taken as supporting the old Paul, I will examine the major relevant texts.

The Statement of Facts and External Matters: 1.11–2.14

After presenting himself and his opponents (1.1–9) and defending his character (1.10—"Am I seeking to please humans?"), Paul undertakes a lengthy narrative of his persecutions of the church, his conversion, his early travels, his meetings with the leaders in Jerusalem, and his subsequent disagreements with Peter in Antioch. If we date the letter itself to the early 50s, the events described in the narrative took place roughly twenty (persecution and conversion) and ten (the most recent trip to Jerusalem) years earlier.

Why would Paul choose to relate these events, some of which predated the present crisis by twenty years and none of which directly involved the Galatians? Part of the answer lies in his rhetorical model, which required that all parties understand the facts and external matters, that is, the background, of the dispute (no. 4 above).

In the narrative itself, which offers a fascinating glimpse into the internal dynamics and tensions of the early Jesus-movement, two themes predominate: first, a vigorous defense of Paul's gospels and, by implication, his authority (no. 6 above); and, second, the independence of his mission to the Gentiles (no. 4). In developing the first theme, Paul goes to great lengths to demonstrate that his gospel came from a divine revelation and not from any human source:

> the gospel which is preached by me is not human. For I did not receive it or learn it from any human source but rather through a revelation of/from Jesus Christ. (1.11).

To back up this claim, he points to himself as the most unlikely of all candidates for such a revelation, for it happened while he was persecuting the church! In the background we are probably safe in assuming that Paul's opponents in Galatia, as elsewhere, must have challenged his authority on various grounds, including the charge that his gospel was a mere human invention.[7]

In the second theme, the issue is Paul's freedom to preach his law-free gospel to the Gentiles. Here Paul is anxious to report that the leaders in Jerusalem had given their full approval:

- They placed no restrictions on him (2.6).

- Once they saw that he had been entrusted [by God] with the gospel to the uncircumcised, James, Peter/Cephas, and John gave him the right hand of fellowship, that is, as a sign of their approval.

- They resisted efforts by "false brethren" to limit Paul's freedom (2.4–5).

- And, at least by implication, Peter agreed to share table-fellowship with nonobservant, Gentile believers.

- We know from the end of the narrative that the last part of the agreement broke down soon after Peter arrived in Antioch; after initially eating with Gentiles, Peter changed his mind and refused to eat with them. The occasion for this about-face was the arrival in Antioch of "certain men from James" who pressured him into accepting the position of the "circumcision party," the law-observant believers who would not share food with unobservant Gentiles even within the Jesus-movement.

The relevance of all this for Galatia seems clear. Paul's opponents there must have claimed the authority of James (I take the phrase "certain men from James" in 2.12 to mean "people who claimed James's authority"), and probably of Peter too. The apostle seeks to set the record straight: his law-free gospel had been recognized and approved by James and Peter! Those who claimed otherwise are not to be trusted. They are hypocrites (2.13)!

The Legal Definition: 2.15–21

It is difficult to determine whether the passage in 2.15–21 continues the apostle's face-to-face tirade (no. 5 above) against Peter (2.14) or represents a somewhat calmer reflection on the full set of issues regarding the law (no. 1 above) and Gentiles. In either case, the legal terminology is unmistakable. This is also a favorite passage for proponents of the old Paul, for it is framed by two statements (2.16, 21) that appear to undermine the law altogether. The passage is so central that it is worth citing in full, using Gaston's translation as a starting-point:

> (15) We who are Jews by birth and not sinners from the Gentiles, (16) knowing that no one [= Gentile/*anthropos*] is justified by works of the law, but rather by the faith-

fulness of Jesus Christ, we too became believers in Christ
Jesus, in order that we might be justified by the faithfulness
of Christ and not by works of the law, because by works
of the law [paraphrasing Psalm 143.2 which lacks "flesh"]
"all flesh is not justified." (17) But, since seeking to be justified in Christ we ourselves have been found to be
[Gentile] sinners, does it follow that Christ is an agent
of sin? Of course not! (18) For since I am building up what
I once tore down, I commend myself openly as an apostate (*parabatês*). (19) For through the law I have died to
the law, in order that I might live to God. I have been
co-crucified with Christ. (20) I still live, but not really I,
[since] Christ lives in me. What I now live in the flesh,
I live in/through the faithfulness of the son of God,
who loved me and gave himself up for me. (21) I do not
[thereby] annul the grace of God. For since righteousness
is through the law, Christ consequently died as a free gift.[10]

Betz typifies the traditional reading of this passage in reading it as a "denial of the orthodox Jewish (Pharisaic) doctrine of
salvation . . . that this 'justification' can be obtained only by doing
and thus fulfilling the ordinances of the Torah."[8] For him,
"works of the law" is equivalent to "the Torah;" similarly,
"anthropos" and "flesh" (*sarx*) in verse 16 refer to everyone,
Jews included.

Sanders and Dunn represent a certain movement away from
this view. Sanders, speaking of Chapter 3, but with Chapter 2 in
mind, notes that "the problem . . . in Galatians is that of the admission of the Gentiles."[9] And he continues,

. . . the quality and character of Judaism are not in view;
it is only the question of how one becomes a true son of
Abraham. . . . I believe that the reason for which Galatians
3 is seen as Paul's argument against Judaism is this . . .
[I]t is believed to be characteristic of Judaism to hold
such a position, so that Paul's argument is perceived to

be against Judaism. A study of Judaism does not reveal such a position. More to the point, that is not Paul's argument in any case.[10]

Yet a few pages later, speaking of the same passage, Sanders states that Paul "passionately embraced [the view] that Jew and Gentile alike are righteoused by faith in Christ."[11] Dunn recognizes that Paul's thought in Chapter 2 is entirely in accord with Jewish views and that he is "wholly at one with his fellow Jews in asserting that justification is *by faith*."[12] But he, too, goes on to see the passage as directed against a "basic Jewish self-understanding,"[13] which he takes to mean the use of the law to foster an attitude of "a too narrowly nationalistic and racial conception of the covenant."[14]

Gaston's reading, which is reflected in the above translation, takes the passage in a completely different direction. He begins with the observation that "Paul is focused on the Gentiles" and that "the problem . . . [is] the admission of the Gentiles." But Gaston follows the principle all the way through, whereas both Sanders and Dunn, along with many others, manage to introduce the otherwise absent Jews into the conversation. For Gaston (and others) *anthropos* is a typically Pauline term for Gentiles; and the key phrase, "works of the law" (*erga tou nomou*), refers specifically to the ambiguous status of Gentiles under the law and should not to be rendered as "the law" or "Torah." Put differently, the apostle to the Gentiles is writing to Gentiles who are being pressured by other apostles, within the Jesus-movement, to take on circumcision and a selective observance of the law.[15] And to drive home his point, Paul proclaims that even he, the zealous ex-persecutor of the church, has become a Gentile sinner, an apostate (2.18), and that he, like his fellow Gentiles in Galatia, has now been justified by the faithfulness of Christ. In other words, even Paul's case demonstrates that the issue is not the law and Israel but the law and Gentiles.[16] Franz Mussner, with whom we began this chapter, puts it this way: "What he [Paul] wishes to lay low is a Christian pseudo-gospel to which . . . even

Peter had confessed as he gave up table fellowship in Antioch. *. . . In the Epistle to the Galatians Paul absolutely does not enter into dispute with Jews.*"[17]

The Rebuttals: Chapters 3–5

"Many scholars who view the opposing missionaries as Jewish Christians nevertheless see Galatians 3 as Paul's rebuttal of Judaism. But the quality and character of Juda*ism* are not in view."[18] So again Sanders. If we maintain this perspective throughout, the series of arguments directed at the Galatians will begin to yield a new meaning:

- 3.1–5: Paul reminds them of an important historical fact: they were converted (i.e., they received the Spirit, through whom they experienced many things, including miracles—3.2–5) not through doing "works of the law" but through hearing Paul's gospel of faith. Why, then, he implies would they wish to return to their former Spirit-less condition? This first rebuttal also sets out the leitmotif for all of the following arguments—the opposition between "works of the law" and faith. But unlike the older view which takes this as an opposition between Judaism and "Christianity," we will see that the contrast is between Gentiles before Christ and after. This is one of the passages that suggests a prior affiliation of the Galatians to a synagogue before their conversion. The argument makes better sense if at least some of the Galatians were affiliated with synagogues, that is, were doing "works of the law," before Paul came to them.

- 3.6–14: The second rebuttal points to scripture and makes several points in rapid succession: first, that Paul's gospel (God would justify the Gentiles by faith, i.e., outside the law) was predicted long ago in scripture; second, that the key figure is Abraham, who was declared righteous by God "from faith/faith-fulness" (*ek pisteôs*—citing Genesis 15.6) and given the prom-

ise that through him all the Gentiles (*ta ethnê*—paraphrasing
Genesis 12.3) would be blessed; third, that this promise has now
been fulfilled in Christ Jesus (3.14—"so that in Christ Jesus the
blessing of Abraham might come upon the Gentiles"); and
fourth, that the blessing means—here Paul drops his rhetorical
bomb—the release of Gentiles from the curse of the law—
"For all who rely on works of the law are under a curse" (3.10;
again quoting scripture, this time Deuteronomy 27.26—"Cursed
is everyone who does not abide by all of the things written in
the book of the law, and do them"). The implication for the
Galatians is obvious and Paul returns to it repeatedly; by returning to observances of the law, they are placing themselves once
again under a curse.[19] There is no argument here that the law is
by nature unfulfillable and/or that it is a curse for Israel.[20] At
every point, Paul has in mind not Jews but Gentiles.[21] Once
again, the contrast is between Gentiles under the law before
Christ (law/curse) and after (faithfulness/blessing). "Paul
affirms the new expression of the righteousness of God in
Christ for Gentiles . . .without in any sense denying the righteousness of God expressed in Torah for Israel."[22] "In Galatians
the polemic has to do with the entry of Gentiles into the people of God."[23] Verse 7 ("it is men of faith who are the sons of
Abraham") must be read in the light of verse 8 (". . . scripture,
foreseeing that God would justify the Gentiles by faith, preached
the gospel beforehand to Abraham"). No other reading makes
sense of the text.

- 3.15–18: The rebuttal moves next to a legal example, building
  on the previous passage in which Gentiles are represented as legal
  heirs of the promise to Abraham. No one can annul or modify
  a will once it has been ratified. Thus the promise to Abraham,
  which came four hundred and thirty years before the giving of
  the law to Moses, remains alive, though still unfulfilled (until
  Christ). Once again, the contrast is between law and promise.
  Once again, the traditional view holds that Paul thereby annuls
  the law for Israel. But unless he has changed audience (Gentiles)

and vocabulary (the promise to Abraham concerns Gentiles),
the statement in 3.18 ("For if the inheritance is by the law, it
is no longer by promise; but God gave it to Abraham by a promise") concerns only the law and Gentiles.

- 3.19–20: Rhetorical concerns dominate this series of short
  asides or clarifications. Paul needs to explain why the law was
  never the intended path for Gentiles and how he can make the
  outrageous claim (v. 10) that "all who rely on works of the law
  are under a curse." His answers are consistent throughout.
  First, the law was added—to Gentiles—because of their transgressions. The giving of the law to Israel through angels (3.19)
  has no precedent anywhere in Jewish sources, whereas the
  double notion of angelic mediation of the law to Gentiles and
  of the law as negative for them is not uncommon.[24] The traditional view, according to which the law was added to Israel because
  of her transgressions, is a later Christian invention, part of the
  consistent anti-Judaism developed in the second century and
  beyond.[25] But it is not present here. There is no "radically un-
  Jewish position with regard to the Torah" and no "negative evaluation of the mediator Moses."[26] Such a view is possible only
  if we ignore everything he has said before and everything that
  comes after; only if Paul himself has forgotten the Gentiles and
  suddenly, without hint or warning, turned to the Jews.

- 3.21–26: Here Paul reverts to the rhetorical device of the
  deliberately deceptive author. Although he has seemingly pit-
  ted the law against the promises of God (the law leads to
  curse—3.10), he abruptly turns the tables on his audience and
  flatly denies this inference. My point, he says, still speaking of
  Gentiles, is that if the law had brought life (to Gentiles), then
  justification and righteousness would have come by the law. But,
  as he has just demonstrated, for Gentiles the law meant sin, curse
  and death (these are Pauline "facts"). Indeed, Paul could not possibly deny the charge ("The law is against the promises.") if he
  were thinking of Israel. The underlying premise here is the dou-

ble effect of the law—life for Israel, death for Gentiles—a premise well attested in Jewish sources.

- 3.23–25: To further clarify his point, Paul introduces the metaphor of the law as a custodian (*paidagôgos*) until Christ came, until "faith was revealed . . . so that we might be justified by faith/faithfulness." Once again, the "we" must mean Gentiles, Paul's real and implied audience throughout the letter. As for the much-misread custodian, Krister Stendahl and others have pointed out that the *paidagôgos* is not a gentle guide who ushers out the age of the law (3.24f.) but rather, in line with the full thrust of 3.10–22, an unpopular household servant from whose harsh supervision the schoolchildren are released through Christ.[27] The only "radical devaluation of the Law"[28] here is for Gentiles.

- 3.26–29: Here Paul brings his rebuttal full circle. "You Galatians have become sons of God, like Israel. For in Christ Jesus you are all sons of God through faith. (3.26) The promise to Abraham has been fulfilled in Christ; you are the promised heirs of Abraham." And, lest we forget, the content of the promise was that "God would justify the Gentiles by faith" (3.8). As for the baptismal reference and formula ("there is neither Jew nor Greek, neither slave nor free, neither male nor female; for you are all one in Christ Jesus") in 3.28, another favorite among traditional readers, its role in the extended argument is simply, as Gaston puts it, to affirm that "as women do not need to become men . . . so Jews do not need to become Gentiles nor do Gentiles need to become Jews."[29] It is a formula of inclusion, not exclusion. "You faithful Gentiles are now in." In similar fashion, J. Louis Martyn locates Paul's use of this formula strictly within the framework of Paul"s attack on his opponents within the Jesus-movement:

> Wherever the Gentile mission is empowered by God,
> it does not continue the distinction between Jew and
> Gentile. But this focus tells us that Paul is concerned

with two Gentile missions, not with two institutions, church and synagogue. The difference is monumental.

And he continues,

> Taken out of its setting, placed for example in the hands of the imperial church that—leaving the message of Galatians far behind—came to see itself as the true religion, while viewing the synagogue as the false religion, Galatians can be made to say many things, some of them hideous.[30]

▪ 4.1–11: In this rebuttal, Paul picks up several threads from the preceding sections—the lowly status of minors, even though they are heirs to the estate; the law; slavery; and sonship. The human subjects, the "we" (v. 3) and the "you" (v. 8f.) must—still— be Gentiles. Not only is there no reason to suppose that Paul has changed audience, but the descriptions of the circumstances of the Galatians before Christ can only apply to Gentiles: "we were slaves to the elemental spirits of the universe" (v. 3); "you did not know God" (v. 8); and "you were in bondage to beings that by nature are no gods" (v. 8). So, too, with the phrase "those who were under the law" (4.5 and 21), which must also refer to Gentiles. Gaston argues that "under the law," like the related phrase "works of the law," is not a characteristic phrase in Jewish texts for describing the relationship of the law and Jews.[31] In short, this is a precise description of the Galatians' circumstances before Christ—pagans who worshipped false deities but also sympathizers loosely and ambiguously connected with Jewish synagogues. Furthermore, the reference to God's Son as "born under the law," far from meaning "Jesus was a Jew," embodies Paul's notion that Jesus had to be born "under the law" in order to be able to "redeem those under the law," just as in 3.10–13 Christ "became a curse for us [Gentiles], in order to redeem us from the curse of the law." The general idea in both places is that a vicarious sacrifice, involving the suffering or death of one figure, can redeem many who are otherwise hopeless, accursed or enslaved. In 3.13f. Paul makes this clear as can be: Jesus' crucifixion was a curse (he paraphrases Deut. 21.23 ["Cursed is everyone who hangs on a tree"] to prove his point); and the point of the curse/crucifixion was to release those under the curse of the law in order that the blessing of Abraham might come upon the Gentiles! There is no reason whatsoever to suppose that Paul has silently changed his audience and begun to address the Jews in his phrase "under the law."[32]

- 4.21–5.1: After a personal appeal to his authority and correct behavior among the Galatians (see no. 4 above), Paul returns to those "under the law." In 4.9 he expressed his dismay that his converts were returning to their former ways. 4.21 ("Tell me, you who desire to be under the law, do you not hear the law?") must carry the same weight—they are reverting to their former status under the law. What that status means has been the subject of the preceding rebuttals—curse, sin, slavery, ignorance of God, and worship of false deities. But Paul tries one more rebuttal, this time contrasting the law and freedom. As promised, he will use the law (his reading of it) against the law (their reading). Thus he sets out to interpret the story (Genesis 16 and 21) of Abraham's two sons (Isaac and Ishmael; only Isaac, the "legitimate" son is mentioned by name) by two mothers and treats it as an allegory (v. 24).[33] That he should once again focus on Abraham should by this point cause no surprise.

The entire passage has served as a favorite proof-text for advocates of the rejection-replacement view of Judaism, from ancient Christian commentators to the present.[34] One way to approach a rereading of Paul's allegory is to follow the lead of C. K. Barrett. Barrett takes the allegory as Paul's response to his opponent's (mis-) interpretation of Abraham's two sons and their mothers as they relate to the status of Gentiles. We know that these opponents had persuaded the Galatian Gentiles to undergo circumcision in order to guarantee their salvation. In making their case, they may well have cited the story of Isaac and Ishmael. According to what must have been a common reading of the story at the time, only the circumcised Isaac was the legitimate heir.[35] Thus, the opponents would have argued, the Galatian Gentiles had to be circumcised in order to be saved.

Richard Hays, following Barrett, treats 4.21–31 as Paul's exegetical effort to refute the argument of his opponents by standing their reading of the Abraham-story on its head. He characterizes this effort as "hermeneutical jujitsu" and "outrageous." "Unless we suppose that Paul was an insane (or duplicitous) reader, we must credit him with some ironic sensibility."[36] And so on. Paul's position is that the story "warrants the rejection of lawkeeping" and nullifies circumcision "as the definitive sign of covenant relation with God."[37] In a "shocking reversal," Paul associates the Hagar-Ishmael-slavery complex not with Gentiles but with Sinai and the law. "What Jewish thinker," asks Hays, "could propound such an equation?" Finally, Paul links "the Abrahamic covenant to the present reality of his Gentile churches, leaping over and negating the Sinai covenant."[38]

This is potent medicine. How to react? My first reaction is to invoke, yet again, the law that states that if Paul appears to say something that makes no sense in Jewish terms, we are probably misreading him. Second, Hays, like others, appears to suffer from occasional memory lapses regarding the target of Paul's counterargument. As he himself states elsewhere, the refutation is directed at the "anticircumcision gospel"[39] of the opponents, the "Torah advocates" who resisted Paul's "Law-free mission to the Gentiles."[40] He also knows that the apostle is seeking to make "a case for admitting Gentiles into membership among the people of God" and that Paul uses the Abraham story to prove that this "has now come to pass in the Gentile church."[41] How then does it happen that the argument suddenly turns against the Jews, against circumcision for Jews, against the covenant with Israel at Sinai? Where have all the Gentiles gone?

Again, it will be useful to lay out the entire passage:

> (22) For it is written [Gen. 16, 17, 21] that Abraham had
> two sons, one from the slave woman [Hagar] and one from

the free woman [Sarah]. (23) But the one from the slave woman was born according to the flesh, the one from the free woman through the promise. (24) These things are to be interpreted allegorically. For these [women] are two covenants: the one, on the one hand, from Mount Sinai, giving birth into slavery. (25) She is Hagar, for Sinai is a mountain in Arabia. She stands opposite the present Jerusalem, for she serves with her children. (26) But the Jerusalem above is free—and she is our mother. (27) For it is written [Isa. 54.1]:

Rejoice, O barren one, who does not bear,

Break forth into singing and cry out, thou who are not in travail,

For many are the children of the desolate one

More than the one who has a husband.

(28) Now you, brothers, are children of promise according to/after Isaac. (29) But just as then the one born accruing to the flesh persecuted the one [born] according to the spirit, so also now. (30) But what does scripture say? [Gen. 21.10] "Cast out the slave woman and her son, for the slave woman shall not inherit with the son" of the free woman. Thus brothers, we are not children of the slave woman but of the free woman. (5.1) For freedom Christ has set us free. Stand fast therefore and do not submit again to the yoke of slavery.

This is a dense passage, made even more problematic by obvious problems in the manuscripts. In particular, the standard reading of verse 25a ("Hagar is a mountain") makes no sense in any interpretation.[42] What is clear is that the entire passage is framed by 4.21 ("Tell me, you who desire to be under the law . . .") and

5.1 ("For freedom Christ has set us free. Stand fast and do not submit again to the yoke of slavery."). If these two verses concern Gentiles, who are in danger of losing their newfound status, then presumably the intervening material should deal with the same people and the same concerns.

The basic questions here are twofold:

1. Is there any basis for connecting the negative use of Sinai not with Israel, as with Hays and many others, but instead with Gentiles?

2. Does it make sense to take the son of the slave (Ishmael) who is persecuting his free brother (Isaac), as designating not Israel but someone else? Who is persecuting whom? Who are the children of the slave/Ishmael? Who are the children of promise? Who is to be cast out?

Gaston points to a series of Jewish texts that explicitly connect the giving of the law at Sinai with Gentiles and specifically with Ishmael. One text, the book of Jubilees (15.28–32), justifies the election of Israel, and the nonelection of the Gentiles, on the grounds that Ishmael and his sons did not approach Sinai to take the covenant upon themselves. Here, as Gaston notes, Ishmael is used, at Sinai, "to indicate the situation of contemporary Gentiles living outside the covenant."[43] Another text, the Targum of pseudo-Jonathan, an expanded translation to Genesis, portrays Ishmael as lording it over his brother Isaac:

> Ishmael said: "It is right for me to be the heir of my father, since I am his first-born son." But Isaac said: "It is right for me to be the heir of my father, since I am the son of Sarah his wife, but you are the son of Hagar, the servant of my mother." Ishmael answered: "I am more righteous than you because I was circumcised when thirteen years old." (Genesis 22)

In this instance, the Targum explains Paul's emphasis on persecution, the choice of Isaac over Ishmael, and the relevance of circumcision. If the troublemakers in Galatia were themselves Gentiles—though this is by no means certain—and were boasting of their recent circumcision as adults, Gaston observes that "Paul must have immediately thought of Ishmael when he heard of them."[44] In other words, the children of slavery, those persecuting (v. 29) the children of the Spirit, are not Israel but the troublemakers opposed to Paul. And his advice to the Galatians is clear: "Cast out the slave and her son" (v. 30 = Genesis 21.10), that is, "expel the agitators and their "children," those who have adopted their views and yielded to their demand for circumcision."[45]

Finally, Gaston proposes a resolution to the difficulties of reading the text by translating the rare verb *sustoichein* in verse 25 as "corresponds to its opposite in the other column." It is obvious enough that Paul has in mind a series of oppositions (sons, mothers, covenants, etc.):

Hagar	*Sarah*
Son (Ishmael)	Son Isaac
From the slave	From the free
Born according to the flesh	Born through the promise
Covenant from Sinai	[Covenant from Abraham]
Giving birth into slavery	Our mother is free
Gentiles before Christ	Gentiles after Christ
Those born according to flesh persecute	Children are persecuted
To be cast out	To inherit

Here the apostle to the Gentiles has turned once again to his favorite biblical character, Abraham, but this time with a new twist. "Yes," he tells his endangered converts, "you are sons of Abraham. But Abraham had two wives and two sons, Isaac and Ishmael. Before Christ you were descendants of the slave woman, Hagar, and her son Ishmael. As Gentiles, outside the covenant at Sinai and before the fulfillment of the promise to Abraham,

you were slaves (4.3, 8) and accursed (3.10). Now you have
been adopted (4.3; cf. Rom. 8.15 where Paul also uses adoption
language to describe the new status of Gentile believers) as
free sons of Abraham and Sarah, like Isaac. But this status can
be lost."

Just as in Romans 11, where Paul warns Gentile believers that
as wild shoots, grafted onto the olive tree [Israel], they can be
easily removed, so here he cautions them that their adoption as
offspring of Sarah and siblings of Isaac can easily be revoked.
Their newly acquired freedom is in jeopardy of becoming, once
again, a yoke of slavery (5.1).[46]

The advantages of this reading are several. It does no violence
to Jewish texts or to common Jewish self-understanding. It
honors the audience of the letter (Gentiles). And it is consistent with the letter's major concerns (to resist Paul's opponents who were seeking to impose circumcision and Torah
observance on Paul's Gentiles). Oddly enough, Hays is one of
the few readers to adopt this reading. "Gentiles once deemed
Ishmaels have now been adopted . . . as "children of promise, according to Isaac" (4.28), fully legitimate heirs of the promise to
Abraham."

> Paul has not merely made a case for admitting Gentiles
> into membership among the people of God; he has
> argued that the Genesis narrative [of Abraham, his wives
> and their sons] is a veiled prefiguration of precisely the
> historical development that has now come to pass in
> the Gentile church.[47]

But for reasons that are not apparent, the old Paul suddenly
reemerges, even in Hays's account; Jews replace Gentiles as
Paul's audience and opponents. "The payoff of this innovative
interpretive strategy is that it allows Paul to link the Abrahamic covenant to the present reality of his Gentile churches, leaping over and negating the Sinai covenant."[48]

- 5.2-6: In his final rebuttal Paul returns to the main issue — circumcision and its negative implications for his converts. "I testify again to every man who receives circumcision that he is obligated to keep the whole law." (5.3) Peter Tomson has shown that the entire sentence is a traditional Rabbinic formula. It appears in several later Rabbinic texts as a warning specifically directed at Gentile converts: "A proselyte who accepts all commandments of the Torah except for one is not accepted."[49] E. P. Sanders argues that these texts imply only that one must accept all of the commandments, not observe them all perfectly.[50] This may well be true, but Paul is using the tradition here to make his own polemical point. It's all or nothing. As Sanders himself notes, it is a threat—"if you start it must all be kept."[51]

- As a final word, Paul returns to the stark antithesis of law and Christ. "I Paul say to you that if you receive circumcision, Christ will be of no profit for you." (5.2) Taken out of context, these words of Paul lead to the view that the law has been annulled for Israel. But read within this letter, they merely reiterate what Paul has claimed many times over in his series of rebuttals: Gentiles are now redeemed from the curse of the law by Christ; to return to the law (i.e., to be circumcised) is to stand again under the curse. And in verse 6 he invokes again a favorite slogan: "For in Christ Jesus there is neither circumcision nor uncircumcision." In context, the slogan can only mean that this distinction, once so fateful for Gentiles, now matters no longer. Unless, that is, Paul comes to a radically different view in Romans 3.1f., where he asks, "What advantage has the Jew? What is the value of circumcision?" And answers, "Much in every way."

A CUTTING REMARK

Before turning to the ethical consequences of his argument in Chapter 5, Paul throws out two final barbs. First, he poses a rhetorical question: "If I am/were still preaching circumcision, why am

I still being persecuted?" (5.11). Three things are clear in this question: Paul feels persecuted over the issue of circumcision; he no longer preaches circumcision; and, at least by implication, at some prior time he did preach circumcision (of Gentiles?). What is not clear is what that prior time refers to. Does it mean that before his conversion, as a Pharisee, he had been a Jewish missionary to Gentiles and had insisted on circumcision?[52] Or had he, even after his conversion, at an earlier stage of his work as an apostle, continued the practice of circumcising Gentile converts, later changing his mind? We cannot know. All we can know for certain is that Paul felt persecuted by his opponents (see 5.11) and argued that their gospel of circumcision (of Gentiles) threatened to undermine the scandal (*skandalon*) of the cross. In this context, skandalon must refer to the resistance occasioned by his gospel that Gentiles were now redeemed by Christ, without circumcision.

As a final jab, Paul indulges in a moment of "savage humor."[53] "I wish those who are unsettling you would mutilate (*apokopsontai*) themselves." Normally translated as "castrate themselves," the Greek verb here points instead, along with the context, to another meaning. For if the knife should slip during circumcision (this is Paul's wicked desire), what would be removed is not the testicles but the penis! The result would thus provide a fitting reward for his enemies' misguided efforts; because of their mutilated bodies, they would be excluded from the community of Israel. It is tempting to imagine here that Paul wanted his converts to recall a passage from Deuteronomy 23.1f.: "He whose male member is cut off (LXX: *apokekommenos*, the same verb used by Paul) shall not enter the assembly of the Lord (*eis ekklēsian kuriou*)." If so, the final phrase, "assembly of the Lord," must have evoked an obvious double meaning— the *ekklēsia* of the Lord (God) of Israel and the *ekklēsia* of the Lord (Jesus Christ). They would be excluded from both.

CHAPTER FOUR

THE LETTER TO THE ROMANS

*In this letter the good news of Paul's gospel for Gentiles is
not part of a polemic against Torah or Israel. Without at all excluding
Jews, he is able to argue very effectively and very passionately that
the inclusion of the Gentiles was always the goal of the Torah.*

Lloyd Gaston

THE CIRCUMSTANCES OF THE LETTER

Thus far our conclusion is that the letter to the Galatians
was not written to, against, or even about Jews; it is
written to Gentiles, about Gentiles, and against apostles within the Jesus-movement. But already in that letter Paul shows an
awareness of potential, or actual, misreadings of his views.

Like Galatians, the letter to the Romans is written to
Gentiles. But, unlike Galatians, it is also written about Jews. It
differs from Galatians in another important respect: its literary
audience was personally unknown to Paul. He had never even
visited that community before writing his letter. The apostle had
created the church in Galatia through his own missionary

efforts; the church in Rome had other, unknown origins. Thus it is difficult to discern against whom Paul is writing. Indeed, given the impossibility of determining what, if anything, he knew of Roman believers (I would not deny that he had received reports through intermediaries) and given our total ignorance of the Roman community in Paul's time, it is probably a wise strategy to avoid unfounded assumptions about Paul's external audience and concentrate instead on the internal, literary audience, that is, those rhetorical figures whom he addresses directly within the letter:

- "Therefore you have no excuse, whoever you are, when you judge others" (2.1).

- "But if you call yourself a Jew" (2.17).

- "I am speaking to those who know the law" (7.1).

For the most part, Paul carries on his argument within the letter. No doubt there were "real" counterparts to these rhetorical figures, but I see no way to identify them as persons or to know much of anything about them.

This strategy for reading the letter as a set of arguments internal to the letter finds support in the unmistakably rhetorical character of the letter as a whole. Even more than in Galatians, Paul here displays and deploys his sophisticated training in the techniques of Greco-Roman rhetoric. Stanley Stowers has shown, in his *A Rereading of Romans*, what unexpected results such a rhetorical reading of the letter can yield and how dangerous it is to ignore its deeply rhetorical character.

At the same time, there can be little doubt that Paul in Romans has in mind concrete issues and persons, almost certainly related to his impending journeys to the church in Jerusalem, whose leaders he had harshly criticized in Galatians, and later to Rome, where news of his work had surely preceded him.[1] This letter is composed after the letter to the Galatians with those issues still very much alive. The relationship between the two letters is revealing—and decisive—for understanding Romans. It is difficult to escape the impression that much of Romans is designed to correct misreadings of Paul's position on certain basic problems—the law of Moses and Israel, the law and Gentiles, Christ and Israel—misreadings stemming in part from the letter to the Galatians itself. " [P]arts of Romans constitute an interpretation of Galatians made by Paul himself."[2] "In Romans . . . one of the purposes is to refute the false rumors that Paul had rejected the Law and his own people."[3] "Paul, for his part, is laboring to refute the charge—whether rhetorical or historical—that *he*, as a promulgator of a startling new teaching incorporating uncircumcised Gentiles into the people of God, has abandoned the ways of the God of Israel."[4] Thus one major difference between the two letters, the lengthy treatment of Israel in Romans 9–11, can be explained as Paul's effort to ward off potential and actual misreadings of his arguments in Galatians. Yes, the law had been a curse and had resulted in enslavement. Yes, the law (and circumcision) has been transcended now by Christ. But all of this applies to Gentiles, not to Israel. His responses, if not his initial arguments, seem reasonably clear. "What is the advantage of the Jews? What is the value of circumcision? Much in every way" (3.1); "Thus the law is holy and the commandment is holy, just and good" (7.12).

As for the issue of Israel's current status—saved or rejected by God?—Paul had not raised this issue explicitly in Galatians. But in Romans, his reply is unambiguous. "Has God rejected his people? By no means" (11.1), "All Israel will be saved" (11.26), "Israel has stumbled but not fallen" (11.11). More important still, Paul sees all of this as part of God's mysterious plan to redeem the Gentiles, according to his promise, and ultimately to save Israel:

> Just as you [Gentiles] were once disobedient to God but now have received mercy because of their disobedience, so they have now been disobedient in order that by the mercy shown to you [Gentiles] they may also receive mercy (11.30f.).

What could have caused this early misreading of Paul's intentions regarding Israel, a misreading that prompts his corrective efforts in Romans? The first observation must be that many of Paul's views were constantly subject to what he regarded as distortions. In 1 Corinthians 5.9, he refers to an earlier letter in which he had warned believers not to associate with immoral persons. And he continues, "I did not mean [that you should avoid] the immoral of the world (the greedy, robbers or idolaters), since that would isolate you from the world altogether, but rather I wrote to you not to associate with anyone who bears the name of brother [i.e., a fellow believer] who is a fornicator, an idolater." Closer to home, he complains bitterly in Romans 3.8 that some have misused his claim that God redeems sinners, concluding falsely that they should continue to do evil things so that more good may come to them. The more sin, the more salvation! "This is what some people claim that we say, defaming us in their speech. Their condemnation is deserved!" No wonder, then, that a somewhat later follower could report that "our beloved brother Paul" wrote things that are difficult to understand (*dusnoêta*), which "the ignorant and unstable twist to their own destruction" (2 Peter 3.15f.).

But what in particular could Paul have said or written to the Galatians that might have led them and others to draw the wrong conclusions about the law and Israel? If I am not mistaken, these are the very same things that have misled readers from Paul's day to the late twentieth century, namely, the seemingly "anti-Israel" passages of Galatians:

- "For all who rely on works of the law are under a curse" (3.10).

- "It is clear that no person is justified before God by the law" (3.11.)

- "For neither circumcision counts for anything, nor uncircumcision, but a new creation" (6.15).

Taken as universal statements, removed from their immediate context (the apostle to the Gentiles speaking to Gentile converts about Gentiles and the law), these passages could easily (mis) lead readers to the following false conclusions:

- "The law is against the promises of God" (Gal. 3.21).

- "The Jew has no advantage and circumcision is of no value" (Rom. 3.1).

- "We overthrow the law through faith" (Rom. 3.31).

- "The law is sin" (Rom. 7.7).

- "God has rejected his people" (Rom. 11.1).

- "Israel has fallen" (Rom.11.11).

- "Israel stands condemned" (Rom. 11.26).

- "Israel is God's enemy" (Rom. 11.28).

Here we can only assume that such (false) conclusions stand behind the series of rhetorical questions posed by Paul and that at least some of them were already being circulated in Paul's name, citing his own words as their justification. As we shall soon discover, Paul repudiates each and every one of these false conclusions. Indeed, this is the underlying purpose of the letter to the Romans. But his efforts ended in failure. The "anti-Israel" reading carried the day. Until the emergence of the "new Paul" in recent decades, the only readers who have been able to break free from the "old Paul" are the contradictionists,—those who abandon all efforts to find a consistent meaning in Paul and claim that he simply said one thing in Galatians (the anti-Israel passages) and another in Romans (the pro-Israel passages). But their efforts also ended in failure, or rather in an admission of their own failure to make sense of the apostle's thoughts. And the anti-Israel reading still carries the day.

THE AUDIENCE

As with his letter to the Galatians, so also with Romans, the interpretation depends almost entirely on the question of audience.
To whom is Paul speaking? The standard view relies on a
twofold assumption: first, that the community of believers in Rome
consisted for the most part of Gentiles, with a minority of
Jewish converts, and that Paul was addressing tensions between the two (or more) groups; and second, that the apostle to
the Gentiles, departing from his practice everywhere else,
speaks not only to Gentiles but also to and against Jews. This
confusion is further compounded by moving from the alleged Jewish
Christian addressees to a characterization of the letter as a
whole as "a debate between the Pauline gospel and Judaism." Hence
the classic description of W. G. Kümmel. His full statement reads
as follows:

> Rome manifests a double character: it is essentially a debate
> between the Pauline gospel and Judaism, so that the
> conclusion seems obvious that the readers were Jewish
> Christians. Yet the letter contains statements which
> indicate specifically that the community was Gentile-
> Christian . . . the letter characterizes its readers unam-
> biguously as *Gentile Christians*. . . . Even so the Roman
> community is *not purely Gentile-Christian*.[5]

This is a remarkably tangled web of unwarranted assumptions
about the Roman church: illogical inferences; muddled notions
of audience; inattention to rhetoric; and anachronistic categories
(Gentile and Jewish Christians). But it is also the standard
view.[6] What is more, its intentions are obvious. The only truth
in the statement is the observation that "the letter characterizes
its readers unambiguously as gentile [Christians]." The rest, including "Christians," is made up for the sole purpose of rescuing the
"old Paul" for Christianity and for Christian anti-Judaism.[7]
For if Romans, like Galatians, addresses a Gentile audience, on

Gentile issues, including the status of the Jews, the final pillar in the edifice of Pauline anti-Judaism simply collapses.

Following Stowers, I will read Romans as Paul's attempt "to clarify for gentile followers of Christ their relation to the law, Jews, and Judaism and the current place of both Jews and gentiles in God's plan through Jesus Christ."[8] In outline, the letter proceeds as follows:

- 1.1–2.16: opening address by the apostle to his Gentile readers, followed by a portrait of Gentile sinfulness and corruption.

- 2.17–4.25: lengthy conversation with a fictive Jewish teacher, viewed as Paul's competitor for Gentile followers (the teacher is presented in 2.19f. as "a guide to the blind, a light to those who are in darkness, a corrector of the foolish, a teacher of children"); the teacher urges Gentiles to observe certain elements of the Mosaic law, but is himself unable to uphold the law, thus bringing the name of God into disrepute; Paul responds that God has now revealed a new path for Gentiles, not through the law but through Jesus Christ; all of this is laid out in scripture (3.21— "the law and the prophets bear witness to it"); the key figure is Abraham (Ch. 4) , to whom God gave the promise that he would be the father of "many Gentiles;" the promise to Abraham has now been fulfilled in Jesus Christ (5.1).

- Chs. 5–8: Gentiles (the ungodly, sinners) are now "justified," "reconciled," "saved," and "made alive" by the death of Christ, just as through Adam all Gentiles had previously been condemned to death; Ch. 7 depicts the hopeless condition of Gentiles under the powers of the law, sin, and the flesh; Ch. 8 speaks of the new life for Gentiles, released from the powers of sin and flesh and reinforced by the hope of even greater glory to come in the near future (8.18— "I consider that the sufferings of the present time are not worth comparing with the glory that is to be revealed to us").

- Chs. 9–11: Paul speaks as a Jew (11.1—"I myself am an Israelite, a descendant of Abraham, a member of the tribe of Benjamin") to Gentiles about Jews; in this rhetorical tour de force Paul warns Gentiles against arrogance toward the Jews and lays out his view that Israel's temporary disobedience is part of God's plan to save the Gentiles; in the end (soon), God will save all Israel.[9]

Throughout the letter, Paul presents and defends his gospel to the Gentiles (1.5—"to bring about the obedience of faith for the sake of his name among all the Gentiles") as fully laid out in scripture. In one sense, the letter is little more than a Pauline commentary on passages from the Hebrew Bible that deal with the redemption of Gentiles at the end of time.

THE ISSUES AND ARGUMENTS

My discussion of Romans will be guided by four principles: (1) As with Galatians, I will assume that the apostle to the Gentiles remains fundamentally concerned with Gentile believers and Gentile issues; even when discussing Israel and its fate in Chapters 9–11, Paul's audience remains Gentile. As one critic has put it, "This is generally remembered with regard to the Epistle to the Galatians, but forgotten when Romans is considered."[10] (2) I will assume that Paul's experiences in Galatia lie in the background; unless strongly indicated otherwise, his views there will be taken as guidelines for reading Romans. (3) In line with the recent work of Stowers, Elliott, Lodge, and others (including some of Paul's earliest readers in antiquity), I will pay close attention to rhetorical issues in the letter; crucial will be Stowers' reconception of Ch. 2.1–16 as addressing an imaginary Gentile and 2.17–29 as addressing not "the Jews" but an imaginary Jew. (4) I have no intention of writing a full commentary on Romans; as with Galatians, I will concentrate on passages that have traditionally been used to support the "old Paul."

The Jews First and Afterwards the Gentiles: 1.16–17

> For I am not ashamed of the good news [*euangelion*], because
> it is a power which God has to save all who are faithful,
> the Jew first and afterwards also the Greek. For it makes
> known God's merciful justice/righteousness (*dikaiosunē*)
> as a consequence of [Jesus'] faithfulness which leads to
> faithfulness [like Jesus']. As it is written, "The righteous
> one [Jesus] shall live as a consequence of faithfulness"
> (Habakkuk 2.4).[11]

These lines serve as thematic statements for the letter as a whole.
As a result they shape the interpretation of the letter as a
whole—and vice versa. Read within the opening of the letter,
several themes stand out:

- Paul's gospel was declared long ago in scripture (1.2).

- The personal center of the gospel is God's son, Jesus Christ.

- Paul's divinely appointed role is to proclaim this gospel to
  Gentiles (1.5, 13–15).

How, then, are we to read the words in 1.16 ("because it is a
power which God has to save all who are faithful, the Jew first
and afterwards also the Greek")? If Paul regularly defines his gospel
in terms of the Gentiles and if, in Sanders's words, "[I]n Romans
1–4, even taking into account 2.17–29, Paul's view is focused on
the Gentiles,"[12] what are we to make of the apparent inclusion
of the Jews, in this central passage, as targets of the gospel? Does
Paul proclaim here—and only here—that salvation for Jews comes
through faith in Jesus Christ? This is the traditional view:
what is implicit here becomes explicit elsewhere—the law is no
longer valid for Israel; the path to salvation for Gentile and Jew
leads to Jesus Christ. Proponents of the "old Paul" bring this view
with them when they read Romans; they find it corroborated in

1.16; and they weave it into the rest of the letter. Even Sanders, who recognizes that the focus is on Gentiles, summarizes Paul's position as follows: "Jew and Gentile alike are righteoused by faith in Christ."[13]

But this old view is purchased at too high a price. In the first place, the wording of 1.16 states simply that the gospel is God's power to save those who are faithful. Even if we follow the standard translation of *tô pistueonti* ("who has faith"), the words supplied by Sanders and others ("in Christ") do not appear in the text. Once again, proponents of the old Paul are required to complete his sentences in order to squeeze him into the old scheme. Second, the old view regularly posits the ridiculous notion that *pistis* (normally translated as faith) is somehow a Pauline invention, rather than the standard biblical and postbiblical theology of Israel, and that Jews of Paul's time believed themselves to be redeemed by virtue of their own works/deeds. This becomes especially evident in traditional treatments of Abraham (Rom. 4), in which Paul's contention that the patriarch was declared righteous by *pistis* is read as an attack on the supposedly common Jewish view. "That Abraham was justified on the ground of his works was indeed what Paul's Jewish contemporaries were accustomed to assume."[14] But when Paul seeks to clinch his case he quotes scripture, specifically, Genesis 15.6: "Abraham was faithful toward God and this was accounted to him for righteousness." What is more, this same Abraham, always Paul's exemplar of *pistis*, is never presented as "believing in Christ." Third, the phrase "the Jew first and afterwards also the Greek," which recurs in 2.9–10 and 3.9, never signifies the exclusion of Israel but rather the redemption of Gentiles, in accordance with scripture and in fulfillment of the promise to faithful Abraham.[15]

In line with the extended presentation in Chapters 1–4, the point is not that Jews are excluded from anything but rather— this is Paul's radical innovation—that Gentiles are now redeemed through the *pistis* of Christ.[16] God is God not just of Jews but also of Gentiles (3.29). The blessings of Psalm 32 apply not just to Jews but also to Gentiles (4.9). Abraham is the father not just of the circumcised who are faithful [= Israel] but also of those who are faithful without being circumcised [= Gentiles] (4.11–12). God will save not only Israel, but also the Gentiles (11.25–26). These are formulas of inclusion, not exclusion.

If anything, Paul goes out of his way to insist that the Jews retain certain advantages that Gentiles will never enjoy—they are entrusted with the oracles of God (3.2); they are Israelites; to them belong the sonship, the glory, the covenants, the giving of the law, the Temple and the promises; to them belong the patriarchs and of their race, according to the flesh, is the Christ (9.4–5). Fourth and final, Stowers draws attention to the key word, *dikaiosunê* ("righteousness"), in 1.17. Its appearance in the opening thematic statement clearly points forward to the whole of 3.21–4.22, which "tells of how God has demonstrated his impartial righteousness by redeeming the gentiles."[17] For, as Stowers continues, "Paul repeatedly explains the "righteousness of God" by referring to scriptural texts that he believes point to the redemption of the gentiles." "Romans is written as if Paul's gospel to the gentiles were the whole ministry of the good news."[18]

Thus, neither in 1.16–17 nor in the rest of the letter does Paul invalidate the law for Israel or suggest that Israel's faithfulness is to be expressed in Christ. It merely anticipates the inclusive argument of 3.27–31—"Yes [he is the] the God of Gentiles, too, since God is one. And he will justify the circumcised out of faithfulness and the uncircumcised through faithfulness." Here the circumcised must represent Israel. As if anticipating some objection to his radical elevation of Gentiles to a status equal to that of Jews, but apart from the law, he queries, "Am I thereby demolishing the law through this notion of faith?" "Not at all," he replies. "On the contrary, I am simply confirming the law." Put differently, as he makes plain at every opportunity, "scripture lays it all out for you to see, this thing that has now happened to Gentiles."

The Sins of the Gentiles and the Theme
of Divine Impartiality: 1.18–2.16

In Chapters 1–4 and again in 9–11, Paul presents and defends
his gospel under the banner of divine impartiality ("For there is
no hint of partiality with God"—2.11).[19] For him this means that
any form of boasting, by Jew or Gentile, is excluded, for God alone
determines the standing of all humans. At times, Paul does address
Jewish boasting (2.17), but it seems clear that his main concern
throughout is with Gentile boasting. To be sure, he says,
Gentiles in Christ have now been elevated to a status equal to
Jews. But given their previously hopeless condition (i.e., the sins
laid out in 1.18–2.16), they are in no position to boast of this
new status. For this status contains not just the promise of salvation but the threat of condemnation "for every human being
who does evil." What has been won can easily be lost.

There can be little doubt that the catalogue of sins in 1.18-
32 describes the sins of Gentiles and that it does so in recognizably
Jewish terms.[20] The only question is whether Paul turns away from
Gentiles at 2.1 and begins to address Jews ("Therefore everyone who passes judgment is without excuse; for in passing
judgment upon the other person you condemn yourself, because
you, the judge, are doing the very same things"). The traditional
view requires such a change of audience here in order to achieve
its goal, that is, that Paul attacks Judaism as such. Ernst
Käsemann is typical of many. "What follows can be understood only as a polemic against the Jewish tradition which
comes out most clearly and with much the same vocabulary in
Wis [= Wisdom of Solomon] 15.1ff."[21]

But a number of recent critics, among them Gaston, Stowers,
and Elliott, have argued that it makes no sense to see Paul as assail-
ing "a characteristically and recognizably *Jewish* attitude" of smug
judgmentalism.[22] Not only do the Jewish texts cited as evidence that Paul is chastising Jews point in the opposite direction, but the normative view in biblical and postbiblical Judaism
is precisely not one of presumption. The classic proof-text

cited in evidence for Jewish moral superiority and presumption on divine forgiveness, Wisdom of Solomon 15, deals with just this issue. It begins, "Even if we sin we are yours [= God's]," but continues, "but we will not sin, because we know that we are yours." Far from indicating Jewish arrogance, the verse points to Israel's total dependence on divine mercy. As for the normative view of forgiveness in Judaism, Elliott puts it this way: "parallels can be adduced to show that within Judaism the temptation to presume on God's covenantal grace was recognized as a perennial problem, and was combatted."[23] Once again we invoke the rule that excludes any distorted depiction of Judaism. The idea that Jews typically presumed on divine forgiveness and expected to escape judgment is just such a distortion.

Overall there is every reason to assume, with Gaston, that "Rom 1:18–2:16 must then be read as a unit dealing exclusively with the situation of the Gentile world."[24] The verbal links between Ch. 1 and Ch. 2 are too strong to allow the introduction of a new (Jewish) audience.[25] The arguments of 1.18–2.16 "seek to establish that God will accept gentiles, provided they behave toward God and neighbor as the law requires, even if they do not become Jews."[26] Far from being an attack on Judaism, everything in 2.1–16 would have been taken for granted by most of Paul's Jewish contemporaries: it is not hearers of the law but doers who will be just (*dikaios*); some Gentiles know by nature what the law requires. 2.12 ("those who have sinned in a lawless manner shall perish in a manner befitting lawlessness; all who have sinned while living within the law shall have their case judged by the law") is not a universal condemnation of humanity, including Jews, but rather a distinction between the truly wicked and those who live, imperfectly, within the law.

In a lengthy discussion of Ernst Käsemann's treatment of Ch. 2, Sanders notes "how difficult it is to fit Romans 2 into the rest of Paul's thought."[27] He speaks of Käsemann's "tortured exegesis."[28] Sanders's own treatment of the supposed difficulty, that is, that it lacks any "distinctively Pauline imprint," is to propose that the entirety of 1.18–2.29 is taken over by Paul from a typical synagogue sermon. "It is slashing and exaggerated, as many sermons are, but its own natural point is to have its hearers become better Jews . . . *not to lead them to becoming true descendants of Abraham by faith in Christ.*"[29] Here again it is striking to see how close Sanders comes to the new view of Paul, while paraphrasing Paul's own words, yet misses it completely. J. C. O'Neill also sees the point of the passage as "a fine appeal to a Jew from a fellow Jew to keep the law which they both profess."[30] Like Sanders, he is unable to fit it into the traditional view, that is, that Paul rejects the law for Israel and so dismisses it as a later interpolation.

But there is another solution to these difficulties.[31] The tortured exegesis and apparent inconsistencies disappear altogether; Ch. 2 fits neatly into the rest of Paul's thought; there is no reason to suppose that Paul has introduced material but failed to shape it to his own point of view;[32] there is no anomaly in Paul's insistence that doers of the law will be declared just;[33] the "distinctively Pauline imprint" emerges clearly; there is no "anti-Judaic thrust" and no "sharpening of Paul's attack on the Jews;"[34] and there is no gap between Ch. 2, where Paul highlights Gentiles who do the law, and Ch. 3, where he criticizes a Jew who flaunts it — all of this is accounted for and is fully consistent with everything else in Chapters 1–4, on the assumption that Paul does not reevaluate Jewish descent from Abraham to mean their acceptance of Christ and that his argument with the Jews is only that they have failed to recognize Paul's gospel, namely, that God has now fulfilled his promise to Abraham regarding the Gentiles, in Christ and outside the law.

Jews and Also Gentiles—Paul's Debate with a Jewish Teacher: 2.17–4.25

- 2.17: Here Paul turns his attention to a Jewish presence in the crowd: "You there, who call yourself a Jew." Stowers's setting of the scene makes good rhetorical sense:

> [H]e spots one of his competitors in the crowd, a Jew
> who has committed himself to teach the gentiles about
> the Mosaic law. Paul knows that many gentiles in the
> audience have been attracted to such teachers and
> decides that he can best continue his missionary appeal
> by provoking a debate with the other Jewish teacher in
> front of his gentile audience (2.17–4.21).[35]

This entire section is a favorite among traditional readers of Paul who see it both as a frontal attack on Judaism and an accurate portrait of Jewish hypocritical boasting about their privileged position before God. Käsemann calls it "a concrete attack on the Jews."[36] C. E. B. Cranfield, in his two-volume commentary, holds that for Paul "all contemporary Jews are guilty" of stealing, adultery, and robbing temples.[37] And so on.

Such conclusions are far removed from what Paul says and how he says it. The point here is not that the law is by nature unfulfillable or that it is misguided or that all Jews consistently disobey the commandments. The setting is competition between two particular Jews—Paul and a nameless Jewish competitor for Gentile followers. Paul's goal is to undermine the credibility of his competitor by pointing to his hypocrisy—he does (steal, commit adultery, rob temples) what he urges his Gentiles followers not to do. And as a result, the name of God is brought into disrepute (2.24). All this is a typical example of rhetorical exaggeration when attacking one's opponents. What is more, Paul is not addressing "the Jews" but a specific (imaginary and caricatured) Jewish teacher.[38] This teacher emerges not from Paul's experience of actual Judaism but from the repertoire of rhetorical diatribes. He is the pretentious and hypocritical teacher of philosophy, the Stoic or the Jew in name only, one whose message cannot be trusted because his own behavior belies the message.[39] Paul must have this image in mind when he addresses his Jewish competitor: "You there who call yourself a Jew."

The upshot of this diatribe is not that the law is in any way deficient, but that the proper Jewish stance toward the law is one

of dutiful obedience. "Reading 2:17–29 as a set of proposi-
tions about the sinfulness and depravity of Jews in general or all
Jews constitutes an egregious misreading."[40] The issue is not Jewish
culpability but rather Jewish accountability. By virtue of possessing
the Torah, the Jewish teacher knows what is required.[41] In this
respect, 2.17–24 fits smoothly into the flow of the argument from
2.13 ("it is not hearers of the law . . . but doers who will be justified") through 3.1ff. ("What advantage has the Jew? What is
the value of circumcision? Much in every way!"). Paul is lecturing
his imaginary Jewish competitor on how he or she should
observe the law. And, as will soon become clear (3.21—"Now
the righteousness of God has been revealed apart from the
law"), he is also announcing that a new way has been opened for
Gentiles through Jesus Christ. The former path of becoming proselytes and observing the law has been shut down. Indeed, as he
argues in Galatians and later in Romans, it had never led
Gentiles to their desired goal anyway.

- 2.25–29: How this verse and what follows can be turned into "an
  anti-Jewish thrust" or treated as Paul's dismissal of circumcision
  "as irrelevant because of circumcision of the heart"[42] remains an
  impenetrable mystery. Few Jews of Paul's times would have
  disagreed with his assertion that "if you become an apostate (*parabatês*) from the law, your circumcision becomes uncircumcision." The Greek *parabatês* is a strong word; the RSV version, "if
  you break the law," hardly conveys its full thrust. In any case, the
  weaker RSV version makes no sense within ancient Judaism. No
  Jew would have agreed that a mere breaking of the law amount-
  ed to a renunciation of circumcision.

"In this regard, Paul was hardly radical or innovative. . . . The
theme 'circumcision of the heart' come directly from the Jewish
scriptures and many varieties of ancient Judaism emphasized it."[43]
Nor is there any need to posit a Jewish belief "that circumcision
as such has saving force."[44] This was simply not a common
view among ancient Jews.

As for the remainder of the discussion, which asserts that those (Jews) who become apostates from the law will be judged by those (Gentiles) who are uncircumcised but nonetheless keep the requirements of the law, Paul adds nothing new. Here one is reminded of a passage in the Jewish writer, Philo of Alexandria (a contemporary of Paul), that makes exactly the same point—divine impartiality leads to unexpected results. Speaking about the fate of Jews and proselytes (Gentile converts) at the final judgment, Philo foresees a stunning reversal of expectations:

> The proselyte, exalted aloft by his happy lot, will be gazed at from all sides ... while the nobly born (Jew) who has falsified the sterling of his high lineage will be dragged down and carried into Tartarus. Thus may all, seeing these examples, be brought to a wiser mind and learn that God welcomes the virtue which springs from ignoble birth (Gentiles), that he takes no account of the roots (Jews) but accepts the full-grown stem, because it has been changed from a weed into fruitfulness.[45]

It is clear that neither Paul nor Philo had any interest in denying the law. Paul simply carries forward the theme of divine impartiality: God will reward the non-Jew who does the law and punish the Jew who turns aside. Stowers remarks that "Paul's thinking ... may not have been convincing to most Jews in antiquity."[46] But Philo, at least, would have nodded his assent.

- 3.1–9: The rhetorical questions in 3.1 represent a typical Pauline procedure: following an argument that appears to lead to one (false) conclusion, he reveals the correct (unanticipated) response. Most modern readers have fallen into his trap.

Paul anticipates a negative answer to the questions, "What, then, is the advantage of the Jew? What is the benefit of circumcision?" But he surprises his audience with a vigorous affirmative, "A great deal in every way!"[47]

As for the remainder of this section (3.3–9), the reading that makes the most sense is that Paul is still preoccupied with the standing of Gentiles and that he is building toward the dramatic climax of 3.21—"Now the righteousness of God has been revealed apart from the law." There is no universal indictment of the Jews. The "promises" (*logia*) of God entrusted to the Jews refer to the Jews' role as a light to the Gentiles, a point on which Paul has already insisted that the teacher has failed. But the failure of some Jews does not add up to a charge that God is unfaithful. Here Paul and the teacher are in agreement. In line with biblical texts and with Paul's own scenario in Chapters 9–11, God unveils a mystery in which the failure and the resulting punishment of "some Jews" (3.3) serves to restore Israel and to redeem the Gentiles.[48] In this sense, 3.5 ("But if our wickedness serves to show the justice/righteousness (*dikaiosunê*) of God") merely anticipates the mystery of Ch. 11, in which God causes Israel to stumble in order to save the Gentiles—and Israel. For as Sam Williams[49] and Stowers[50] have shown, God's righteousness in Romans means above all the "just settlement of the situation of the gentiles."[51]

Thus the final question in the dialogue (3.9a—"Are we Jews at a disadvantage?"), often taken as contradicting 3.1 (Jews enjoy many advantages), merely confirms Paul's consistent message, that is, some Jews have sinned and will be justly punished, a message that would hardly have raised an eyebrow among Paul's Jewish contemporaries.[52] In contrast to those who would see 3.9b ("all are under sin") as the climax of Paul's thought and as a universal condemnation of humanity, Stowers notes wryly that "[a]ncient readers . . .would have more likely greeted the statement with a yawn than a gasp."[53] He comments further "that much of the discourse about God, Israel, and the gentiles appears prominently in ancient Jewish writings."[54] Paul himself quotes Isaiah 52.5 (LXX) to the effect that "the name of God is blasphemed among the Gentiles because of you (Israel)." Again Paul quotes (1 Corinthians 14.25) a passage from Isaiah 45.14–25 in which the Gentiles are led to repentance as a result of witnessing

God's salvation of Israel. The same pattern appears in Ezekiel 36.23–26 (LXX). What is novel with Paul is not the close connection between God's punishment and ultimate redemption of Israel, leading to Gentile repentance, but rather the order of events. For as Chapters 9–11 make clear, it is now the redemption of the Gentiles that will cause Israel to repent and be saved!

- 3.10–20: Gaston has proposed that the entire section of Romans, from 1.18 to 3.20 (excluding 2.17–29, where Paul addresses the Jew directly), can be read as an indictment, not of Jewish sins but of the Gentile world. Paul's concern throughout is to establish the case that Gentiles, like Jews, are accountable for sinning and thus stand under judgment. This is the negative aspect of the inclusion-motif of Paul's gospel. The positive aspect follows in 3.21ff. Several considerations support this view. First, the series of biblical indictments cited here, when read in context, turn out to be directed not at the righteous of Israel but at her enemies. Psalm 14 (cited here in 3.10–11) addresses the fool who says "There is no God," and speaks of "the evil-doers who eat up my people." The adjacent Psalm (LXX), though not quoted by Paul, identifies the enemies repeatedly as *ta ethnē*, that is, Gentiles. "The catena is not evenhanded but excoriates Gentile sinners."[55] Decisive here is the summation in verses 19–20, which uses language characteristic of Paul's description of Gentiles. As we have already seen in our reading of the letter to the Galatians, phrases like "those under the law," "works of the law," and "through the law comes knowledge of sin" point exclusively toward Gentiles. If we look for clues that Paul is talking about Judaism, we will be disappointed. To see Paul as debating Judaism is neither intelligible nor plausible.[56] The claim in 3.20 ("no human being will be justified in his sight by works of the law") is a virtual quotation of Galatians 2.16. The standard reading of the verse as a condemnation of the Mosaic law itself or of Judaism as a religion of "works-righteousness" has been roundly rejected by most recent interpreters.[57] Instead, we need to understand that the issues and the audience in the two letters are the same—Gentiles are now justified in a new way (3.21ff.).

Stowers has added an important insight concerning the setting of Paul's treatment of Gentile sins—and redemption. Paul's primary concern is with what is happening now, at the end of history, not with elaborating a theory of human history as such. His language thus "fits within that broad and varied Jewish discourse known as apocalyptic." Within that Jewish discourse, and thus in Paul, we find not just that the "Gentile problem" will be resolved at the end of history but that the end will be preceded, and recognized, by a "time of crisis and tribulation before the arrival of the new age."[58] No one doubts that apocalyptic thinking clearly underlies the urgency of Romans 9–11; but it permeates Chapters 1–8 (and 12–15) as well. Paul remains an apocalyptic thinker throughout.

- 3.21–30: Here Paul develops the positive side of divine impartiality—or, which amounts to the same thing, the redemption of the Gentiles. Of course, the traditional reading of this crucial text discovers, once again, Paul's rejection of the law, not just for Gentiles but for Israel as well. But a number of recent interpreters take it in an entirely new direction. "[T]he theme of the inclusion of the Gentiles clearly appears as permeating the entirety of these verses."[59] "Romans 3.21–31 is clearly about the inclusion of the Gentiles."[60] The evidence is overwhelming:

  - Throughout Galatians and Romans, the phrase "God's righteousness" (3.21— "Now the righteousness of God has been revealed") means the redemption of the Gentiles.

  - The righteousness of God is manifested in the faith/faithfulness of Jesus Christ (3.22); "the formula relates primarily to the inclusion of the Gentiles. . . . Paul understood the faith of Jesus Christ to be the fulfillment of the promise given to Abraham. . . . Christ

kept faith (= faith of Christ) with the divine promise by opening the doors to the Gentile nations."[61]

- Both here and in Galatians, the phrase "for all who have
  faith" (or: "are faithful") refers to Gentiles, either exclusively
  or primarily; in either case, the dominant theme is the redemption of Gentiles.

- The words of 3.23, "for all have sinned and fallen short of the
  glory of God," recapitulate the catalogue and the climax of
  Gentiles sins in 1.18-3.20.

- Divine righteousness reveals itself by passing over former
  sins (3.25f.), that is, the sins of the Gentiles.[62]

- The "human being" (*anthropos*) in 3.28 who cannot be justified by works of the law, but rather by *pistis*, must be the Gentile,
  since "works of the law" is a Pauline tag for Gentiles.

- The brief rhetorical dialogue in 3.29 ("Is God the God of Jews
  only? Not also of the Gentiles? Yes, also of the Gentiles") is
  an inclusion-formula; it cannot be read in any other way.

- A similar inclusion-formula appears in 3.30, which sums up
  the theme of divine impartiality and inclusiveness—"God will
  justify the circumcised out of *pistis* and the uncircumcised through
  pistis"; the use of different prepositions (*ek* and *dia*) with *pistis* points to different paths for Jews and Gentiles, while
  pistis means not faith in Christ, as the traditional view must
  assume, but the *pistis* revealed to and embodied in Abraham
  (Ch. 4).

"Boasting" in 3.27 (the root is *kauch-*) is a distinctively Pauline
term. In its various forms it occurs some fifty-four times in his
letters and only four times in all other New Testament writings
combined. Its connotations are not uniformly negative for

Paul, although peculiar RSV translations hide this fact. In
Romans 4.2, for instance, the RSV renders the word as "boasting" but in the very next chapter (5.2) as "rejoicing," that is, "in
our hope of sharing in his glory." For Paul it would appear
that some things merit boasting, while others do not.

The question in 3.27a ("What then becomes of our boasting?")
has stood as another pillar in the structure of the old Paul. For
Käsemann, the reference to boasting provides the "final polemical edge to the theses of vv. 21–26 . . ." and is directed at the question of the prerogative of the Jew. "[T]he law in fact throws a
person back upon himself and therefore into the existing world
of anxiety about oneself, self-confidence, and unceasing self-
assurance."[63] The exclusion of boasting (3.27b) means the end
of the law.

Stowers has proposed a new reading of 3.27 that takes seriously the rhetorical character of the passage as diatribe; Paul is
still engaged in his dialogue with the Jewish teacher.[64] The
question in 3.27 comes not from Paul but from the boastful teacher
(2.19–22). In contrast to the teacher's "condescending pride over
against gentiles" and following Paul's claim that Gentiles are now
justified apart from the law, "it comes as no surprise when the
teacher says . . . , 'Where does that leave our boasting?'" Paul's
answer (3.27—"It [boasting] is excluded . . . through the teaching of *pistis*") merely recapitulates the essence of 3.21–26: God
has opened a new way for Gentiles, no longer through "works
of the law" but through *pistis*. Paul has now dealt a double
blow to the teacher's mission: first, because the teacher himself
was unfaithful to the law (2.17–24); and, second, because a
new way, apart from the law, has been revealed (3.21–26). Paul
has unfolded his assault on the teacher in stages. In Chapters 5–8,
he will complete his task. There he will contend that the law was
never the path to righteousness for Gentile sinners. For "the law
came in to increase the trespass (of Adam)"—5.20. The law—
in itself holy, just, and good—meant death for Gentiles (7.7–12).
"Now there is no longer any condemnation for those who are in
Christ Jesus" (8.1). Throughout, the apostle to the Gentiles main-

tains his focus on Gentiles. The issue is the law and Gentiles. The setting is competition for Gentiles between Paul and the teacher. The target is not Israel but Paul's pretentious and fictive fellow Jew.[65]

- 3.31-4.23: Pursuing his rhetorical analysis, Stowers traces the continuing dialogue between Paul and the teacher into the discussion of Abraham. Two points are essential. First, the questions posed ("Are we destroying the law through this *pistis*?" and "What should we say? Have we found Abraham to be our forefather according to the flesh [i.e., by his own efforts]? For if Abraham was justified by his works/deeds, then he has reason to boast"[66]) come from the teacher. Second, Abraham is Paul's answer to the first question and, by extension, to the claim in 3.21 that the law and the prophets bear witness to the revelation of God's righteousness apart from the law. Both here and in Galatians, Abraham is the scriptural guarantor of Paul's gospel to and about the Gentiles. Here again, Paul stands in a long line of Jewish thinkers, beginning with the book of Genesis, who see Abraham as the key to understanding the ultimate salvation of Gentiles.

Paul's reply to the teacher makes four basic assertions:

1. Abraham is the father of Jews (of course) and also of Gentiles (4.10ff.)—of Gentiles because God declared him righteous before his circumcision (4.10–11) and of Jews because he received circumcision as a sign of his *pistis* ("likewise the father of the circumcised who are not merely circumcised but also follow the example of *pistis* which Abraham had before he was circumcised"). Acceptance of the Gentiles is the basic theme. Paul backs up his claim with a reference to Psalm 32 ("Blessed are those . . . Blessed is the one") and asks, "Is this blessing pronounced only upon the circumcised or also upon the uncircumcised?" (4.6–8) Following on the inclusion formulas of 3.29f., Paul marshals more biblical proof for his case. Abraham is par-

ticularly useful, however, since he is able to show that God justified him before his circumcision. Thus the passage in 4.14 ("If
it is the adherents of the law [Israel] who are to be the heirs,
faith is null and void"), often taken as rejecting the law, can only
mean that the heirs are not limited to Israel. This is clear not
only in what comes before (4.11–12: Abraham is the father of
the circumcised as well as the uncircumcised) but in what
comes after (4.16: the promise rests not only on adherents of
the law but also on those who share the *pistis* of Abraham). But
it is not just in Genesis that the relationship between Abraham,
righteousness, and the redemption of the Gentiles appears. Isaiah
51.1–8 (LXX) and Sirach 44.19–21 similarly make the same
connections.[67] There is no evidence to support the widely
held belief that "Paul's Jewish contemporaries were accustomed to assume . . . [t]hat Abraham was justified on the ground
of his works."[68] Thus the need for Gaston's insistence that "[e]very
interpretation of Paul that is based on a misrepresentation of
Judaism is to be rigorously excluded."[69]

2. The righteousness that God reckons to Abraham in response
   to the patriarch's *pistis* manifests itself as the future redemption of the Gentiles. This righteousness comes to Abraham as
   a promise to be fulfilled in the future. Abraham trusts the
   promise that he would be the father of many heirs despite the
   fact that he was already an old man (4.16–21, which summarizes the biblical account of Genesis 15). The promise of
   Genesis 15.5 (i.e., that Abraham would have many descendants;
   the text does not mention Gentiles) is then interpreted by Paul
   via Genesis 17 (4.17) where the promise is repeated, this time
   with specific mention of the many heirs/descendants as
   Gentiles (*ethnê*). The RSV obscures this point by translating
   ethnê in 4.17–18 as nations.

3. The fact that Abraham, the father of the Gentiles, was justified before his circumcision establishes Paul's claim that
   Gentiles, as the co-descendants of Abraham, were never

intended to be justified by the law. Thus neither the teacher nor Abraham has any ground for boasting, that is, in works (4.2— "if Abraham was justified by works he has something to boast about"). In fact, says Paul, Abraham was justified for his trust in God and only then was circumcision added as a sign (4.11). Thus the teacher has no ground for insisting that Gentiles attain justification by circumcision. The only issue in view is the teacher's message regarding circumcision and Gentiles. Paul has already made clear his view of circumcision and Israel: "Circumcision is of value if you obey the law" (2.25) and "What is the value of circumcision? A great deal in every respect" (3.1f.).

4. The connections among the three major themes—Abraham, *pistis*/faith, and Gentiles—point finally to a fundamental aspect of Paul's thinking. He clearly thinks of *pistis* as defining the relationship between God and Israel. At the same time, while recognizing the biblical roots of *pistis*, I have moved increasingly toward the view that Paul thought of faith/faithfulness primarily with reference to Gentiles. The reason for this is that he also thought of Abraham, the faithful patriarch, primarily with reference to Gentiles. Thus, when he says, "those who are of faith (*ek pisteôs*) are blessed with faithful Abraham," he clearly means Gentiles.[70] Beyond this, I am inclined to read such classic texts as Romans 1.16 ("I am not ashamed of the gospel: it is the power of salvation for all who have faith, the Jew first and then the Greek") and 3.21f. ("Now the righteousness of God has been manifested apart form the law . . . the righteousness of God through the *pistis* of Jesus Christ for all who have faith") in the same manner. Almost thirty years ago, George Howard made a similar claim. But it has been slow to take effect. "This means that through the loyalty [*pistis*] of Christ to the Promise all the Gentiles are brought into the scope of God's grace."[71] "Particularly in Romans and Galatians, the formula [*pistis christou*] relates primarily to the redemption of the Gentiles . . . Paul understood the faith of Jesus Christ to be the fulfillment of the promise given to Abraham. . . . Christ kept

faith (= faith of Christ) with the divine promise by opening the doors to the Gentiles."[72]

The New Life for Gentiles: 5.1–8.39

"These chapters [5–8] attempt to show how gentiles obtain obedience and life in Christ."[73] They complete Paul's argument with the teacher, now adding the final blow. The law was never meant to lead Gentiles to justification; instead, under the power of sin, it led to death and condemnation. Now, in Christ, Gentile believers have peace with God (5.1), acquittal and life (5.18), and hope of salvation (8.24).

The "we" in 4.24f. and 5.1 means Paul and his Gentile believers. Their anticipated adoption as sons (8.23) recalls Galatians 4.5, which similarly speaks of Gentiles receiving adoption as sons.

Chapter 7 has long been cited against this reading. It has often been taken as the crowning argument in Paul's case against the law as such and for all people. The "I" language has given rise to the view that the person speaking (7.5—"our sinful passions, aroused by the law, were at work in our members for death") is Paul himself and that the passage offers us his compressed spiritual autobiography. The law could not and cannot be fulfilled. Only Jesus Christ can deliver us, that is, Gentiles and Jews, from "this body of death" (7.24).

Such is the traditional and the still dominant reading. According to Krister Stendahl, few Pauline texts have been more thoroughly and persistently misinterpreted.[74] The results are clearly visible not only in theological treatises and biblical commentaries but in vernacular translations as well. At its worst, this powerful misreading has succeeded in turning Paul's views into the very opposite of his stated intention.

But is there any reason to suppose that Paul has radically changed his view of the law in just a few chapters? Conversely, is there any reason to suppose that he has lost sight of his main theme, that is, the law and Gentiles? None at all. In the first place, W. G. Kümmel's 1929 essay on Romans 7, which argued against an autobiographical reading, has now been widely accepted. But if not true of Paul, is it perhaps still true of other Jews, that the law leads to sin and death? Stowers has shown that everything about Ch. 7, including its context, points to Gentiles as the ones for whom the law has meant death, just as in Galatians the law had led to curse and condemnation for Gentiles (Gal. 3.13—"Christ has redeemed us [Gentiles] from the curse of the law"):

- The language points to the rhetorical technique of speech-in-character (*prosôpopoiia*), or impersonation, where the speaker presents the circumstances and trials of someone altogether different from himself.[75]

- The underlying idea of the chapter—"I know what I should do but cannot do it"—was a commonplace in Greek literature, beginning with Euripides' Medea. About to slay her children, she laments, "I know that what I am about to do is evil but passion is stronger than my reasoned reflection."[76] Thus the formulas in 7.15 ("For I do not do what I want, but I do the very thing I hate") and 7.19 ("For I do not do the good I want, but the evil I do not want is what I do") evoke not Jewish but specifically Greek dilemmas. "Paul unsurprisingly uses Greek traditions to convince Greeks."[77]

- Finally, modern readers were not the first to discover the apostle's rhetorical use of characterization.[78] Nilus of Ancyra comments,

  God forbid! The divine apostle is not speaking of himself when he says [Rom. 7.23], "I see another law in my members taking me captive through sin." Rather these things are spoken by a person representing those who are troubled by fleshly passions.[79]

And in another fragment, Nilus identifies this person as "belonging to those who have lived outside the law of Moses" [i.e., Gentiles]."[80]

When Paul summarizes his gospel in 8.1f ("There is now no condemnation for those who are in Christ Jesus. . . . For the law of the spirit of life in Christ Jesus has set me free from the law of sin and death"), he does so using language characteristic of Gentiles throughout the letter. When he speaks unambiguously of the law and Israel, he never uses terms like condemnation and death. Moreover, there is a strong thematic continuity between Chapters 1–4, which emphasize the disobedience, the sins, and the redemption of the Gentiles, and Chapters 5–8, which speak of their new life in Christ. Any other reading goes against the grain not just of the entire letter but of every Jewish understanding of the law. Little wonder that older Jewish readers of Paul spoke with dismay of his profound distortion of Judaism. But if, as more recent readers have discovered, Paul is not speaking of the law and Israel, that issue disappears. Still, the damage has been done. "I believe it a great tragedy that generations of Christians have seen Jews through these dark lenses."[81]

The Redemption of the Gentiles and the Salvation of Israel: Romans 9–11

Chapters 9–11 present the final hurdle for all readers. They have become the ultimate test piece. For the old view, the stumbling block is that Paul's most positive affirmations about the law and Israel's salvation appear here:

- "To the Israelites belong the sonship, the glory, the covenants, the Temple and the promises; to them belong the patriarchs and of them in a human sense is the Christ" (9.4f.).

- "Has God rejected his people? By no means!" (11.1).

- "All Israel will be saved" (11.26).

For proponents of the old view, these assertions must be either ignored or treated as an expression of Paul's hopeless state of confusion. "We have left out of consideration these three chapters (9–11), chiefly because they do not form an integral part of the main argument . . . we are inclined to ask if he has not got himself into inextricable (and needless) difficulties by attempting to salvage some remnant of racial privilege for the historic Israel."[82] "He likewise contradicts himself when discussing the . . . problem of Israel's reluctance to accept the gospel. In Romans 9 he resorts to the extreme explanation of divine hardening which takes place regardless of any of man's doings (9.6–23), whereas he in the very next chapter puts all emphasis on Israel's own notorious disobedience."[83]

For advocates of the new Paul, the argument must be that these chapters constitute not a digression but the rhetorical climax of the letter and that they are consistent not just internally but with the rest of the letter. Krister Stendahl commented in 1963, "To me the climax of Romans is actually chapters 9–11, i.e., his reflections on the relation between church and synagogue, the church and the Jewish *people*—not 'Christianity' and 'Judaism.'"[84] Since that time, a broad consensus has emerged on this point, so that even readers not inclined toward the new Paul now take it for granted. "A closer study reveals the fact that there are very many features of chapters 1–8 which are not understood in their full depth until they are seen in the light of chapters 9–11. . . . these chapters may be seen to be an integral part of the working out of the theme of the epistle."[85]

As for the alleged contradictions and inconsistencies, only a careful analysis of the text will reveal whether the apostle is yet again "involved in intellectual difficulties."[86]

- 9.1–2: From this point on Paul transforms the tone of his appeal. "I have great sorrow and unceasing anguish in my heart. For I could wish that I myself were cut off from Christ for the sake of my [Jewish] brethren"(9.2f.). "Brethren, my heart's desire is that they [Israel] may be saved" (10.1). What are we to make of this outpouring of pathos? Why the dramatic emphasis on Paul's Jewishness?

Two forces are at work throughout these chapters. First, Paul is still following rhetorical conventions. Quintilian and other ancient teachers of rhetoric urged their students to make use of emotional appeals, precisely at the climax of their address:

> The prime essential for stirring emotions of others is ... to feel those emotions oneself. ... We must identify ourselves with the persons of whom we complain that they have suffered grievous, unmerited, and bitter misfortune, and must plead their case and for a brief space feel their suffering as if it were our own.[87]

In short, Paul's goal in these highly personal outpourings is to evoke compassion for his fellow Jews and to plead their cause.[88] It is also true that Paul speaks here as a Jew. His readiness to sacrifice himself echoes the words of Moses (Exodus 32.32), who appeals to God, "But now, if you will forgive their [i.e., Israel's] sin—and if not, blot me, I pray, out of your book which you have written." To conceive Paul's self-representation as a Jew is essential, for it reveals that "the letter does not contrast Jews and gentiles but Jews who represent opposing solutions to the gentile problem. ... To ignore this is to risk an egregious misreading of the letter."[89]

In 9.6–10.21 we plunge into the heart of the matter. Paul is deeply troubled over his people, Israel. What the problem is, he does not reveal immediately. Indeed, throughout Chapters 9–10, he will proceed slowly, even deceptively, tempting his readers in one direction but setting them finally on a completely different course. Paradox and reversed expectations lurk at every corner as Paul creates and then dissolves the tensions among three fundamental assertions: Israel has failed to achieve what it sought (11.7) and has stumbled (11.11); there is no divine injustice in any of this; and God has not rejected his people, Israel.

- The implied question in 9.6 ("It is not as though the word of God has failed") opens the discussion by recalling the earlier debate with the Jewish teacher. Paul is revisiting familiar territory. The teacher had objected ("Does their faithlessness nullify the faithfulness of God?"—3.3–5; "Do we overthrow the law by this faithfulness?"—3.31) that the redemption of the Gentiles had invalidated God's commitment to Israel. Such appears repeatedly to be the unmistakable consequence of Paul's gospel. Yet he will not allow this conclusion. We need to examine how he works his way out of this seeming impasse. In doing so, we need to remain mindful of two features of his efforts. One is, as Gaston puts it, that he "gives too many answers to his own questions . . . any one of which would suffice, but which are not completely consistent in their plurality."[90] I take his redundancy here to be a measure of how difficult he perceives the task to be. The other feature is his conscious decision to adopt the rhetorical strategy of the unreliable author. He misleads in order to convince. We need to avoid falling into his trap.

- 9.6b–13: The first attempt makes use, once again, of the promise to Abraham and Sarah. We know from elsewhere (Galatians 3 and Romans 4) what the promise means to Paul—the adoption of Gentiles as children of Abraham as God's free act. Gentiles are no longer the unchosen children of Esau (9.13, quoting Malachi 1.2f.) whom God hated but have become the children of the promise. There is no hint here of Gentiles displacing Israel. The theme is inclusion. "Paul does not dispute but emphatically affirms in these verses the common Jewish concept of the election and that by grace alone."[91]

- 9.14–23: The second attempt pursues the notion of divine freedom (9.14—"Is there injustice on God's part?") by defending not so much God's absolute power to do as he chooses, though this lies in the background, but rather God's mercy (quoting the words of Moses in Exodus 33.19—"I will have mercy on whom I have mercy"). To illustrate his point, Paul cites the case of Pharaoh. The hardening of Pharaoh's heart represents not an act of capricious power but an expression of divine mercy. Paul quotes God's words to Pharaoh (Exodus 9.16—"I have raised you up . . . so that my name may be proclaimed in all the earth") in order to show that even then God had in mind the redemption of the Gentiles through Israel. God's wrath is always justified ("Who are you, a human being, to answer back to God?"—9.20). But that is not the point. For God shows his wrath and power "in order to make known the riches of his glory for the vessels of mercy . . . even us whom he has called, not from the Jews only but also from the Gentiles" (9.23). Once again, the formula ("not only . . . but also") points to inclusion, not exclusion.

- 9.24–29: The third attempt consists of a series of biblical proof-texts to support the notion of inclusion. The passages from Hosea (2.23; 1.10) point to God's merciful election of non-Jews ("Those who were not my people I will call 'My people'"—Hos. 2.23). Those from Isaiah (10.22f.; 1.9) demonstrate God's mercy in preserving a faithful remnant within Israel ("If the lord of hosts had not left us children, we would have fared like Sodom"—Isa.1.9). Surely Paul must also have had in mind the immediately following verses (Isa. 10.24–25) in Isaiah in which God offers reassurance—"Thus says the lord of hosts, do not fear my people . . . for my anger will cease in a little while." Stowers comments that "Paul was presenting no novelty in viewing the remnant as an instrument of Israel's salvation, but was following patterns typical of later Jewish scriptural interpretation."[92] The prophetic verses "confirm that God's promises remain valid."[93] The remnant-motif is the guarantor of God's unbreakable covenant with Israel.

- 9.30–33: The fourth attempt pushes the reader to the brink. "Gentiles who did not pursue righteousness have attained it

... but Israel who pursued the righteousness which is based on the law did not succeed in fulfilling that law" (9.30f.). Here, surely, Paul preaches the exclusion of Israel and her replacement by Gentiles. Israel did not pursue righteousness through faith but through works. They stumbled over the stone placed by God. "Behold, I am laying in Zion a stone that will make men stumble, a rock that will make them fall; and he who believes in him will not be put to shame" (9.33 citing Isaiah 28.16—but conforming neither to the Hebrew text nor to the LXX). "They have a zeal for God but it is not enlightened" (10.2). "Israel's pursuit of the law *ex ergôn* ["by works"—9.32] was blindness to the law's witness to Christ. Its legalistic misunderstanding and perversion of the law and its rejection of Him were inextricably intertwined."[94]

Against this reading stand several considerations: (a) neither here nor anywhere else does he criticize Judaism as a religion of legalistic works-righteousness; (b) the issue here is righteousness, and righteousness for Paul means, as 10.4 emphasizes, God's plan for the redemption of Gentiles; (c) the Zion-stone placed in Israel's way, which virtually all readers have taken as Israel's refusal to believe in Christ, need not be taken as a christological reference, any more than the reference to the Zion-deliverer in 11.26 (quoting Isaiah 59.20f.); much more likely is it a reference to the Torah itself (in 9.33)[95] and to God (in 10.26). On this last issue, Paul Meyer makes the following observation: "no commentary known to me departs from the unanimous decision that for Paul this stone is Christ. There is no more striking example in the Pauline letters of a crucial exegetical decision made on grounds extrinsic to the text itself."[96]

In similar fashion, Gaston's exasperation with traditional readings conveys some sense of their inherent implausibility:

> How is it that people can say that chapter 9 deals with the unbelief of Israel when it is never mentioned? ... How can people say that Paul teaches the divine rejection of

Israel in chapter 9 when he later expressly says the opposite (11.1)? . . . How has Romans 9 been turned into an
anti-Jewish polemic?[97]

- It is now possible to give at least a partial answer to Gaston's questions. The fatal flaw in the traditional reading lies in its failure
to recognize Paul's rhetorical strategies, in particular his use of
the unreliable author. He has set the trap and many have fall-
en prey. "Generations of Christian readers have taken the apostle's bait without ever feeling the spring of the trap."[98] "[T]he
unreliable implied author lured the readers into this trap." "It
is, indeed, *a position which Paul has encouraged through the deliberate ambiguities of his own argument.*"[99]

- Chapter 10 both continues the emotional tone of Paul's appeal
and advances the theme of Israel's failure. "They did not submit to God's righteousness. For Christ is the *telos* of the law with
respect to righteousness, for all who believe" (10.3f.). This is a
classic proof-text for the "old" Paul: Israel's misstep was its refusal
to believe in Christ as Israel's salvation; Christ spells the demise
(*telos*) of the law for all, Gentile and Jew. This is the "dark
Manichaean shadow across the pages of Paul and of his commentators" spoken of by Paul Meyer.[100]

There are major difficulties with the traditional, and virtually unanimous, reading. The first concerns the translation of *telos*.
To render it as "termination" or "cancellation," while lexically possible, is highly irregular. Nonetheless it has been widely adopted by many modern readers, that is, "Christ brings the law to an
end."[101] Referring to Käsemann's translation of *telos* as termination, Meyer laments that "[T]his is a kind of ultimate example
of the way in which the understanding of 10:4 depends on
decisions that one has made elsewhere."[102]

More generally, *telos* generally means something like goal, end-
point, or fulfillment. What is more, Paul has already made it clear
that for him the law is still very much a valid and living reali-

ty. Thus to read the phrase as "Christ is the goal of the law" is to place it alongside passages like Romans 3.21 in which Paul speaks of God's righteousness as revealed apart from the law, "although the law and the prophets bear witness to it."

The second difficulty relates directly to the term *righteousness* (*dikaiosunê*). In the same passage (3.21), it means, using almost identical language, the redemption of the Gentiles. It must mean the same thing here (10.4). Christ is the goal of the law in terms of righteousness, that is, "with respect to God's plan to redeem the gentiles."[103] And the phrase "for all who believe" refers, as we have see repeatedly, to Gentile believers. "The point that seals the case is the observation that Paul repeatedly explains the 'righteousness of God' by referring to scriptural texts that he believes point to the redemption of the gentiles."[104]

As for the remainder of Chapter 10, the dense material in 10.5–17 lays out the apostle's sense of the relationship between his preaching to the Gentiles and their belief. The biblical passages quoted in 10.18–21 (Psalm 19.4; Deuteronomy 32.21; Isaiah 65.1; Isaiah 65.2) continue to lay the trap for inattentive readers and prepare the way for the dramatic reversal of expectations in Chapter 11.

At the same time, our reading of 10.4 (and 9.33, the Zion stumbling stone) begins to clarify the character of Israel's failure. First, it has nothing to do with accepting Christ as Israel's saviour. What Israel missed was understanding the goal of the Torah as it relates to Gentiles. "The righteousness of God for Gentiles, which is the goal of the Torah, has now been manifested, and it is the failure of Israel to acknowledge this which is what Paul holds against them."[105] Second, the mention of the divinely placed stumbling stone should alert us to another Pauline surprise. "The argument in chaps. 9 and 10 deliberately refrained from revealing Paul's assumption all along that Israel's 'stumble' is not so as to fall."[106] Israel's stumble is neither fatal nor of her own doing. God caused Israel to stumble. Suddenly, 9.16a ("It depends not on human will or effort") emerges in a new light. Nor is her misstep an unfortunate accident. It is part, an essential part, of the divine plan to redeem the Gentiles and to save Israel (9.16b— "but upon God's mercy"). But as Paul's use of Deuteronomy 32.21 ("with a foolish nation I will make you angry"—10.19) and Isaiah 65.1 ("I have been found by those who did not seek me"—10.20) begins to unfold, the expected order of events will be reversed. It is no longer, first Israel, then the Gentiles. In these final days ("now") it is the Gentiles first, then Israel (Ch. 11).

In 11.1–36 Paul approaches his dramatic conclusion with a stunning reversal. Israel's salvation is now dependent on the fate of the Gentiles! The new motto is Gentiles first and afterwards Israel.

"The 'true' implied reader of Romans 9–10 turns out to be the reader who can accept the thesis of 11.1 without reservation as the correct conclusion from reading chaps. 9 and 10!"[107] If so, the vast majority of modern readers must be classified as false. To them, the affirmation of 11.1a comes as a surprise. "I ask, then, has God rejected his people? By no means!" The unveiling of this riposte occupies the remainder of the chapter, with a basket full of surprises.

Paul's first line of defense, in 11.1–11, is to claim that he himself is an Israelite and a descendant of Abraham. The point of this reply is far from clear, until we realize that for Paul (11.2— "God has not rejected his people whom he foreknew") Israel's status as chosen by God is an absolutely unshakable fact. Together with Abraham (to whom God gave the promise regarding the Gentiles), Israel represents God's steadfast commitment to "reconcile the world" (11.15), "to bring in the fullness of the Gentiles" (11.25), "to save Israel"(11.26), and "to have mercy on all" (11.32).

Paul's reference to himself as evidence that God has not rejected his people leads him naturally to his next argument, the faithful remnant within Israel (11.2b–10). The identity of this faithful remnant, chosen by grace, has been a matter of considerable debate. Among traditional readers, the answer is simple and obvious—the remnant is the total number of Jews who have come to believe in Jesus Christ. This is yet another version of the rejection-replacement view. But Paul does not say this. And he has already stated twice that God has not rejected his people. More likely is Gaston's suggestion that the remnant refers to figures like Paul, that is, those Jews who proclaimed the Torah's message regarding the Gentiles.[108]

But it would be a cheap victory, and a misreading of the remnant-theme itself, for Paul to rescue God's promise to Israel by arguing, "Well, not everyone in Israel has refused to believe in Christ. There are people like Peter and me." Beyond this, P. E. Dinter has shown that the remnant-motif served a positive function in ancient Judaism. The faithful remnant is a tool used by God to bring salvation to all of Israel.[109]

The next surprise is that the rest of Israel, precisely the part that failed to obtain what it sought (11.7), plays a critical role in the divine plan of salvation. Before unveiling this paradox, however, Paul reiterates two earlier themes. The first is that the hardening, the failure to obtain, the stumbling, are all the work of God! "God gave them a spirit of stupor" (11.8, quoting Isaiah 29.10). The second, contrary to what the unreliable author has again led his readers to expect, is that Israel has stumbled but not fallen. "So I ask, then, have they stumbled so as to fall? By no means" (11.11a).

Here we must note that it is not only Paul's implied readers (in the letter) who have drawn the wrong conclusion, despite his threefold protest, but virtually all modern readers as well. "Despite Paul's clear restatement of his belief that the majority 'tripped' against the stone (11.11) and did not fall, commentators never cease speaking of Israel's 'fall.'"[110] Here at last Paul really does appear to contradict himself. The RSV translation of the passage (Isaiah 28.16) quoted by Paul in 9.33 reads as follows: "Behold, I am laying a stone in Zion that will make men stumble, a rock that will make them fall." Whereas in our passage (11.11), he claims that Israel stumbles but does not fall! The Greek in 9.33 uses the phrase *petran skandalou*; the term *skandalon* is never used to refer to a fall but only to a trap, a snare, or a stumbling stone. In any case, its placement is always deliberate.

Once again, the RSV translation of a crucial passage has been determined by factors outside the text.

Finally, in 11.b–32, Paul drops his guise as an unreliable author and unfolds the ultimate paradox. Räisänen typifies many readers in finding what comes next as "something quite unexpected after 9:6–11:10."[111] He has fallen into the trap, despite the fact that Paul himself had pointed the right way in his earlier citation of the prophet Hosea: "Those who were not my people I will call my people" (9.25). What emerges now is the positive role of Israel's disobedience in the divine plan of salvation. As with Pharaoh (9.17), God has hardened Israel—or rather a part of Israel (11.25)—in order to bring salvation to the Gentiles. He repeats this refrain, with slight variations, many times over:

- "through their trespass salvation has come to the Gentiles" (11.11a).

- "their trespass means riches for the world" (11.12a).

- "their defeat (*hêttêma*) means riches for the Gentiles" (11.12b).

- "their loss (*apobolê*; the RSV translates this as rejection, clearly reading the rejection-theory into rather than out of the word) means the reconciliation of the world" (11.15).

- "branches were broken off so that I might be grafted in" (11.19).

- "a hardening has come upon a part of Israel, until the full number of the Gentiles come in" (11.25b).

- "you have now received mercy because of their disobedience" (11.30).

- "they have now been disobedient in order that by the mercy shown to you" (11.31).

In other words, it is Paul's belief that God has not only

caused Israel's stumbling and disobedience but has done so intentionally, in order to bring redemption to the Gentiles! Why it should have to happen this way Paul does not say. The best he can do is point to biblical passages in which God promises to create a people from those who were not a people (9.25f.; 10.19f.) and to juxtapose these passages with others that speak of Israel's disobedience (10.21, quoting Isaiah 65.2) and jealousy of those who are not a nation (10.19, quoting Deuteronomy 32.21—"I will make you jealous of those who are not a nation; and with a foolish nation I will make you angry"). This is the divine mystery revealed to Paul and spelled out in 11.25–36:

> I do not want you to misunderstand this mystery, my fellows: a hardening has come upon a part of Israel [or: a provisional hardening has come upon Israel], until the full number of the Gentiles shall come in. Thus all Israel will be saved. . . . O the depth of the riches and wisdom and knowledge of God! How unsearchable are his judgments and how inscrutable his ways.

Throughout these chapters, Paul remains fully aware that his readers may still be tempted to treat the redemption of the Gentiles (and Israel's stumble) as the final chapter of the story, even though he has already made it known that the ultimate stage involves the salvation of Israel too. That much has already been established repeatedly and with sufficient variation to make the point indelibly:

- "I ask, then, has God rejected his people? By no means!" (11.1).

- "God has not rejected his people whom he foreknew" (11.4).

- "So I ask, then, have they stumbled so as to fall? By no means!" (11.11).

- "The gifts and the call/election by God are irrevocable" (11.29).

- "From the point of view of election, they are beloved on account of the patriarchs" (11.28b).

What is new in the story, the mystery as Paul calls it, is that the redemption of the Gentiles and the salvation of Israel are intimately intertwined. Their final destinies are interdependent. But not as Israel had expected, for at the end it is the Gentiles first, then the Jews, thus reversing the formula ("the Jews first, then the Greeks") in the early part of the letter:

- ". . . so as to make Israel jealous" (11.11b).

- "how much more will their [i.e., the Gentiles'] full inclusion mean" (11.12b).

- "I magnify my ministry in order to make my fellow Jews jealous and thus save some of them" (11.13f.).

- "their [i.e., the Jews'] acceptance will mean life from the dead" (11.15).

- "the other, if they do not persist in their unbelief, will be grafted in . . . how much more will these natural branches [i.e., Israel] be grafted back into their own olive tree" (11.25f.).

- "I want you to understand this mystery, brethren: a hardening has come upon a part of Israel, until the fullness of the Gentiles comes in, and so all Israel will be saved" (11.25).

- "in order that by the mercy shown to you [Gentiles] they may also receive mercy" (11.31).

By this point Paul's readers must have been out of breath. In fact, Stowers has shown that the image of a foot race underlies the entire section, beginning in 9.30 ("Gentiles attained righteousness").[112] The Greek word *hēttēma* (11.12), normally translated as failure (see the RSV), has another quite ordinary common meaning—defeat in an athletic contest; *paraptôma* in the same verse commonly refers to a misstep in a foot race; the theme of stumbling but not falling (11.11) carries the image forward; and the jealousy-motif functions to correct Israel's misguided zeal in the race. In a reversal of all previous expectations, Gentiles now coach Israel in the art of running. But, and this is Paul's point, Israel will finish the race. Then comes the End.

Two final points emerge from Chapters 9–11. First, as Stendahl,[113] Gaston,[114] Stowers,[115] and others have noted, Paul issues a warning in these chapters—a warning not to Jews but to Gentiles. In the lengthy metaphor of the olive tree, he likens Gentiles to branches unnaturally grafted onto Israel's tree and cautions them to avoid any sign of arrogance. "Do not boast over the branches [of Israel]. . . . Do not become proud" (11.18, 20). "Lest you [Gentiles] become arrogant" (11.25). In the long run, of course, this warning was ignored. Gentile Christianity, in the name of Paul, did become arrogant, proud, and boastful against Israel and in the process completely abandoned Paul's gospel.

The second point concerns the pivotal claim in 11.26 ("all Israel will be saved") and the following citation of Isaiah 59.20f. ("The Deliverer will come from Zion"). This is the second divine mystery, the culmination of the letter. By now the reader knows that the fullness of the Gentiles will come in, that their redeemer is Jesus Christ, and that Paul is the apostle of this message. Still uncertain, however, is the identity of Israel's saviour. One possible clue lies in the language of 9–11, especially 10.18–11.36. "It is stunning to note that Paul writes this whole section of Romans (10.18–11:36) without using the name of Jesus Christ. This includes the final doxology (11.33–36), the only such doxology in his writings without any christological element."[116] Is the Deliverer of 11.26 (= Isaiah 59) Jesus Christ, as the traditional view has always maintained? Certainly not originally in Isaiah, where it must be God.

Krister Stendahl observes that in 11.26 Paul states simply, "All Israel will be saved." "Paul does not claim that when the time of God's kingdom, the consummation, comes Israel will accept Jesus as Messiah."[117] "Paul does not explicitly say that all Israel will ultimately believe in Jesus as Christ, but simply that they will be 'saved.'"[118] Mary Ann Getty comments that

> it is far from certain that Paul makes a christological ref-
> erence here when he speaks of the Deliverer. . . . Paul has
> not referred to Christ since Rom 10:17 and . . . the dox-
> ology of 11:33–36 is the only theological, rather than chris-
> tological, doxology in Paul.[119]

Getty notes further than when Paul uses the verb *rhuomai* ("I save"), God is always the subject and that the mention of covenant in the verses from Isaiah ("and this will be my covenant with them when I take away their sins") indicates God's covenant with Israel. "In our context, Paul speaks about the fulfillment of the promise made to Israel, not a discontinuous covenant."[120] ". . . the whole process of Israel's salvation at the limit of history will be the work of God."[121] "[T]he one who has been imposing his will on Israel and the Nations will save Israel. God is the one who hardens Israel and God will be the deliverer."[122]

In the end, it seems difficult to avoid two fundamental results: first, Chapters 9–11 establish Paul's claim that God has not reject-ed his people, Israel; and, second, Israel's salvation, while not unre-lated to the redemption of the Gentiles through Christ, does not take the form of embracing Christ. "For Paul, Jesus is neither a new Moses nor the Messiah, he is not the climax of . . . God's deal-ings with Israel, but he is the fulfillment of God's promises concerning the Gentiles."[123]

A Final Note: 15.7–18

These final verses sum up the entire letter. What is striking about the language here is the total focus on the Gentiles. Paul makes two assertions that deserve attention. First, in 15.15f., he writes,

"I have written to you very boldly in part by way of a reminder, because of the grace given me by God to be a minister of Christ Jesus to the Gentiles." Bold indeed, unless we read Paul in the old manner, in which case he falls in line with the anti-Judaism of later Christianity. Second, in 15.18 he writes, "I will venture to speak of nothing except what Christ has wrought through me to win obedience from the Gentiles." Does this not state, in this final summation, that for Paul Christ is the redeemer of the Gentiles—exclusively?

That is bold. Nonetheless, it is what Paul says. Indeed, he introduces his summation with a strikingly similar claim:

> For I tell you that Christ became a servant from the circumcised to show God's mercy on behalf of God's truthfulness, that is, to confirm the promises to the fathers/patriarchs, so that the Gentiles might glorify God for his mercy.

I am inclined to take the final clause as describing the content of the promises. Christ's mission was to confirm God's truthfulness by bringing Gentiles to glorify God, in fulfillment of the promises to the fathers/patriarchs. "Romans is written as if Paul's gospel to the gentiles were the whole ministry of the good news."[124]

CHAPTER FIVE

LOOSE ENDS

The Covenant is both theirs and ours!
The Epistle of Barnabas

CHAPTER FIVE—LOOSE ENDS

I have tried to put forward the strongest possible case for my position. One danger in taking such an approach is that we come to believe too fully in the strength of our case. Indeed, one recurrent theme among proponents of the new Paul are sentences that begin with phrases like "How can they [i.e., the defenders of the old Paul] say that. . ." or "It is astonishing that. . ." and so on. Do these sentences represent the rhetorical hyperbole of an embattled minority? Or perhaps the excessive zeal of a recent convert? A better way might be to characterize them as typical expressions spoken from within a new paradigm. For once we step outside the old paradigm, all is lost. Once we begin to question not just specific texts or issues within that paradigm, but the paradigm itself, nothing in the old model makes sense.[1]

Nonetheless, there are always loose ends. I will deal with some of them briefly.

There is no absolute unanimity among defenders of the new Paul on every detail. On the issue of whether Paul repudiates the law of Moses and rejects Israel as the people of God, however, there is something close to general agreement. The answer, echoing Paul himself, is No. Paul puts forward no criticism of the law as such. The law remains in effect for all who are circumcised. The key here has been the recovery of the immediate context of Paul's letters and, with it, the realization that his targets/opponents are not Jews/Israel but anti-Pauline apostles within the Jesus-movement. But on the question of whether Israel's salvation lies in Christ, whether Paul regarded Jesus Christ as the Messiah of Israel, there is no such agreement. Neil Elliott and W. D. Davies, who argue forcefully against the view that Paul abrogates the law, still describe Israel's failing as her refusal to accept Jesus as her Messiah.[2] As noted earlier, Stanley Stowers hesitates, settling on the formula of "separate but related ways of Jews and gentiles."[3] My own view, along with that of Lloyd Gaston and Krister Stendahl, is that Paul, in maintaining the validity of the law and the constancy of God's promises to Israel, does not envisage an End-time conversion of Israel to Christ. I find no evidence in Paul's letters to reach such a conclusion. Moreover I find it to be inconsistent with Paul's affirmation of the law's continued validity for Israel. As to the question of whether we can speak of Paul's *Sonderweg* or special path for Israel, I am rather of the view that it is the other way around. For Paul, Israel's salvation was never in doubt. What he taught and preached was instead a special path, a *Sonderweg*, for Gentiles.

It might be argued that Paul identified Israel's path to salvation with his own life history (that is, conversion to Christ) or, failing that, with the pattern of other Jews like Peter, James and the "pillars in Jerusalem" who had embraced Jesus as their Messiah. But he does not say so. Ironically, the only place where Paul urges others to follow him occurs in the letter to the Galatians (4.12), in which he urges his Gentile converts to imitate Paul the Gentile!

"Become like me, for I have also become like you [i.e., a Gentile]!" In any case, he never suggests that Peter and the others should abandon their practice of the law. Whether Paul himself regularly observed the law is unclear. "It may be that Paul wanted to have it both ways, to understand himself as an apostate in relationship to his Gentile converts but as a loyal son of Israel in relationship to Jews."[4]

The very existence of Peter and others like him, that is, law-observant Jews who accepted Jesus as the Messiah of Israel, has caused some to doubt the plausibility of the new Paul. Why this should be is not clear. Whatever Paul understood by Peter's gospel to the circumcised (Gal. 2.7), Paul preached his own gospel to the uncircumcised. Perhaps he saw Peter's gospel (that is, Jesus as Israel's Messiah) in terms of the faithful remnant spoken of in Romans 9 and 11. But we do not know. What we do know is that he regards his Jesus-movement opponents as enemies and that he mentions Peter and the others only once, in Galatians, and then only for the purpose of validating his law-free gospel to the Gentiles. Otherwise they play no positive role in his thinking. "To the degree that it affords hospitality to the False Brothers and their circumcision party . . . the Jerusalem church is nothing more [i.e., for Paul] than an earthly entity, limited to the *present* time and even analogous to the *present* evil age."[5] Paul's enemies lay within the Jesus-movement, not outside.

Charges of inconsistency and self-contradiction have hounded Paul from antiquity to the present. A pagan critic of the third century C.E. accused him of "variable and contradictory utterance."[6] Even in mainstream Christian circles one finds an awareness of similar charges and a spirited defense of the apostle against them. It is only fair to admit that Paul himself must bear partial responsibility for the problem. In 1 Corinthians 9.22 he describes his missionary methods: "I became a Jew to Jews, so that I might gain Jews; to those under the law I became like one under the law . . . to those outside the law I became like one outside the law . . . I became weak to the weak." But this is a description not of inconsistency or self-contradiction but rather of Protean adaptability.[7] Conversely, the burden must fall on those who have persisted in reading Paul while ignoring the common rhetorical culture of the apostle and his readers. Such ignorance, coupled with a refusal to locate him within his own immediate setting, leads inevitably to the charge of inconsistency.

An angry passage in 1 Thessalonians 2.14–16 has often been cited as evidence either of Paul's inconsistency or of his "real" view of the Jews:

> You, brethren, became imitators of the churches of God in Christ Jesus which are in Judea; for you suffered the same things from your own countrymen [i.e., Gentiles] as they did from the Jews, who killed both the Lord Jesus and the prophets, drove us out, and displease God and oppose all men by hindering us from speaking to the Gentiles so that they may be saved—so as always to fill up the measure of their sins. But God's wrath has come upon them at last.

There are at least two solutions for dealing with the difficulties posed by this text. The first, which has recommended itself to many readers, including a number who have no interest in the new Paul, is that the passage is a later interpolation and thus not Pauline at all.[8] The second is to read it within the context of Paul's life. We know that Paul encountered opposition to his mission from Jews outside the Jesus-movement. We know that one of the precipitating issues was the status of Gentiles. We know that the author of this passage is using language borrowed from the Hebrew Bible: for example, "The Lord, the God of their fathers, sent persistently to them by messengers . . . but they kept mocking the messengers of God, despising his words, till the wrath of the Lord rose against his people, till there was no remedy" (2 Chronicles 36.15f.). In other words, the notion of divine punishment for Israel's sins was not a Pauline invention. In any case, there is no hint of a general condemnation of Israel. "Here, as elsewhere, Paul's condemnation of fellow Jews falls upon those who have actively opposed his law-free mission to gentiles."[9] Finally, we must reckon with the possibility of development in Paul's thinking from the time of this early letter to the time of Romans, a period of at least five years. The key terms (wrath of God, sins, salvation of the Gentiles, Jews, the End) will remain constant, but in 1 Thessalonians there is no sign of the remarkable recombination that we find in Romans. If such a development did indeed occur, we can only conclude that Paul's early outburst was put to more creative purposes at a later date.

Paul's mode of argumentation was consistently biblical. Here he was at one with all other Jews and, later, Christians. That is, he was convinced—and he sought to persuade others—that his gospel was clearly and precisely laid out in Scripture. At virtually every turn he cites a biblical text, often several. Many have seen his interpretations of these texts as willful, even perverse. The literary critic Harold Bloom is beside himself. "Paul is so careless, hasty, and inattentive a reader of the Hebrew Bible that he very rarely gets any text right."[10] He speaks of Paul's "will to power over a text," of "weird exegesis" and of "plain howlers." Here Bloom is surely in agreement with other Jewish readers of Paul, ancient and modern. They do not find Paul's exegesis convincing. But two considerations are in order. First, when Bloom speaks of "normative Jewish interpretation,"[11] he is just wrong. There was no such thing, only competing schools and traditions. Second, the work of Gaston, Stowers, and others has shown that Paul's reading of biblical texts is by no means as weird as Bloom would have us believe. Rather it is Paul himself who has been misread. Still, it must be recognized that few Jews in antiquity would have accepted Paul's exegetical conclusions. But the reason for this was not that Paul lacked skill as an exegete. The disagreement was not about method. Most Jews simply did not believe his gospel. For this reason alone, his arguments made no sense.

That Paul's thinking underwent significant changes throughout his lifetime is beyond dispute, not just immediately following his conversion/calling but in the later years as well. Recently, Justin Taylor and Etienne Nodet have proposed a development in Paul's christological thought that may have some bearing on my argument. They describe two phases in his thinking about Jesus Christ: at first he identified Jesus as the traditional Jewish Messiah who was about to return; later on he underwent "a profound transformation" and came to see Jesus as Lord.[12] "Messianism . . . has disappeared, or rather, has been transformed: the Messiah has already arrived (resurrection), and 'Christ' becomes a special proper name."[13]

Two questions remain. First, what accounts for the emergence of the new Paul at this point in Western history? Or, to rephrase the question, why have Jews and Christians clung to the old Paul for so long? Second, what difference does it make whether we adopt the new Paul or the old? Is the new Paul in any way relevant for today? The first question is by definition unanswerable in any final sense. It is too broad to allow of certainty. Yet I would hazard a suggestion. For nearly twenty centuries Jews have suffered periodic episodes of hatred, discrimination, and genocide at the hands of Christians (and others). On the Christian side, the anti-Judaism of the New Testament, with Paul at its center, has contributed significantly to this story. Not surprisingly, many Jews came to see Paul—the renegade Pharisee—as the enemy. No great effort was required here, for Jews simply adopted the anti-Jewish image of Paul presented to them by Christians. But with the founding of the state of Israel, in 1948, the story of Jews as a persecuted minority came to an end. For many Jews, Christians were no longer the enemy in the castle. Many Western countries recognized the state of Israel, and by implication its Jewish roots and character, as a living reality. It is within this new framework, I would suggest, that it has been possible for Jewish readers to recover Paul as a Jewish figure and to pry him loose from his anti-Jewish past.

As for Christian readers, it would be convenient, if self-serving, to claim simply that the true Paul has finally emerged. But that is not enough. Instead, my sense is that the Nazi

Holocaust, together with the founding of the state of Israel, account for the possibility of reading Paul in a new way. The issue here is not just, as Lloyd Gaston puts it, that these events should "inspire an apologetic revision of texts written in the past."[14] Rather it is the momentum of several forces that has dislodged the old paradigm from its privileged position, shaken its foundations, and created a space within which a new reading of Paul became possible. Other forces are surely at work, but these two have been fundamental.

Finally, what can we say about the relevance of the new Paul for today? The problem, of course, is that the entirety of Paul's End-time scheme soon became obsolete. In a word, he was wrong. Nothing happened as predicted. Instead, when mainstream Christianity stripped away the apocalyptic setting of Paul's statements about Israel (Romans 9–11), what remained was the image of Israel as disobedient and hardened. This was the price paid in order to wrest Paul from his apocalyptic roots. Such a price was necessary if he was to be made relevant for later, post-apocalyptic Christianity. But for Paul this would have been— or rather, as I have argued, it already was—blasphemous. He had already experienced the false conclusions that could be drawn from his words and he struggled mightily, though unsuccessfully, to defeat them.

In the end, we might decide to conclude that Paul was wrong—period. And put him aside altogether. But for many readers this is not an attractive option. He occupies more than one-half of the Christian Bible. Christianity without Paul is unimaginable. For some, this has meant leaving Christianity altogether and moving into a post-Christian stance. For others, however, it has seemed possible to shake the Pauline foundations of Christianity without destroying the faith completely.

It may seem rash for me, as a nonbelieving "Christian," to venture onto theological territory. I do so because of my conviction that there is more at stake here than mere Christianity. My proposal is that we strip away the apocalyptic framework of Paul's thought in a different way. If we remove this apocalyptic mystery altogether, that is, the notion that in the final days of this era God causes Israel's momentary stumble in order to redeem the Gentiles, we are left with two basic affirmations: one, God's unshakable commitment to Israel and to the holiness of the law (= Judaism); and, two, the redemption of the Gentiles through Jesus Christ (= Christianity).

NOTES

INTRODUCTION

Epigraph: E.R. Dodds, *Pagan and Christian in an Age of Anxiety* (Cambridge, 1965), 34 .

1. From Nietzsche's 1888 essay, "The Antichrist. An Attempted Criticism of Christianity," sect. 42, in *The Complete Works of Friedrich Nietzsche*, vol. 16, ed. Oscar Levy (New York, 1964), 184f.

2. On these so-called enemies of Paul see Gerd Luedemann, *Opposition to Paul in Jewish Christianity* (Minneapolis, 1989), and Wayne Meeks, *The Writings of St. Paul* (New York, 1972), 176–184 ("Paul as Satan's Apostle: Jewish-Christian Opponents").

3. Robert Hamerton-Kelly, *Sacred Violence: Paul's Hermeneutic of the Cross* (Minneapolis, 1992), 11–12. See the discussion of Neil Elliott, *Liberating Paul, The Justice of God and the Politics of the Apostle* (Sheffield, 1995), 67, with references to similar statements in the works of C. H. Dodd and F. W. Beare.

4. Heikki Räisänen, *Paul and the Law* (Tübingen, 1987), 201f.

5. Räisänen, *Law*, 264.

6. The criticisms appear in the reply of Macarius Magnes, a fourth-century Christian apologist; see Adolf Harnack, *Kritik des Neuen Testaments von einem griechischen Philosophen des 3. Jahrhunderts* (Texte und Untersuchungen, vol. 37, no. 4; Leipzig, 1911). Harnack identifies the philosopher as Porphyry, the student of Plotinus. The translation is that of Margaret M. Mitchell, " 'A Variable and Many-sorted Man': John Chrysostom's Treatment of Pauline Inconsistency," *JECS* 6(1998): 93.

7. Mitchell, "Variable."

8. J. C. O'Neill, *Paul's Letter to the Romans* (London, 1975), 16.

9. J. C. O'Neill, *The Recovery of Paul's Letter to the Galatians* (London, 1972), 8.

10. O'Neill, *Galatians*, 86.

11. Mitchell, "Variable," 98. The words appear in Chrysostom's sermon on 2 Corinthians (PG 61.545).

12. See the useful discussion in Stanley K. Stowers, *A Rereading of Romans. Justice, Jews, and Gentiles* (New Haven, 1994), 289f.

13. For a brief and intelligent discussion of reader-response criticism in relation to Paul, see John G. Lodge, *Romans 9–11: A Reader-Response Analysis* (Atlanta, 1996), esp. ix–32.

14. See Elaine Pagels, *The Gnostic Paul. Gnostic Exegesis of the Pauline Letters* (Philadelphia, 1975).

15. See the important treatment of the noncanonical Acts of Paul by D. R. MacDonald, *The Legend and the Apostle: The Battle for Paul in Story and Canon* (Philadelphia, 1983).

16. On the struggle over Pauline authority in the early centuries, see Maurice Wiles, *The Divine Apostle: The Interpretation of St. Paul's Epistles in the Early Church* (London, 1967), and Walter Bauer, *Orthodoxy and Heresy in Earliest Christianity* (Philadelphia, 1971).

17. Stowers, *Rereading*; see also his earlier work, *The Diatribe and Paul's Letter to the Romans* (Chico, 1981).

18. Lodge, *Reader-Response*.

19. Two striking examples of new readings made possible by rhetorical analysis are worth mentioning. Frank Kermode's *The Genesis of Secrecy. On the Interpretation of Narrative* (Cambridge, 1979) is a study of the Gospel of Mark by a nonbiblical specialist. The results are illuminating, and along the way Kermode chastises biblical specialists for ignoring rhetorical analysis. Also revealing is R. Alan Culpepper's study of the Gospel of John, *Anatomy of the Fourth Gospel: A Study in Literary Design* (Philadelphia, 1983), with a foreword by Kermode.

20. Stowers, *Rereading*, 15.

21. Paul Meyer, "Romans 10:4 and the 'End' of the Law," in *The Divine Helmsman: Studies on God's Control of Human Events, Presented to Lou H. Silberman*, ed. J. L. Crenshaw and S. Sandmel (New York, 1980), 64.

22. Quotation from personal correspondence with Lloyd Gaston, cited in John G. Gager, *The Origins of Anti-Semitism: Attitudes Toward Judaism in Pagan and Christian Antiquity* (New York, 1983), 198.

23. Lloyd Gaston, *Paul and the Torah* (Vancouver, 1987), 15; Gaston's

essay appeared originally in *Anti-Semitism and the Foundations of Christianity*, ed. A. T. Davies (New York, 1977).

24. E. P. Sanders, *Paul and Palestinian Judaism. A Comparison of Patterns of Religion* (Philadelphia, 1977), 552 (his emphasis).

25. Sanders, 551 (his emphasis). In his later book, *Paul, the Law, and the Jewish People* (Philadelphia, 1983), Sanders appear to waver somewhat on this issue but to come down finally on the traditional side. "[Paul] seems not to have perceived that his gospel and his missionary activity imply a break with Judaism" (207). This tendency to complete Paul's thoughts in a way that he himself did not is a recurrent and worrisome theme among traditional interpreters.

26. Krister Stendahl, *Paul Among Jews and Gentiles* (Philadelphia, 1976), which includes his famous essay "Paul and the Introspective Conscience of the West," first delivered as a lecture in 1961 and published in English in the *Harvard Theological Review* 56 (1963). Stendahl's more recent and more far-reaching views appear in his *Final Account. Paul's Letter to the Romans* (Minneapolis, 1995).

27. I use these terms in specific ways. "Christian" includes not only those who identify themselves as Christians but also those, like Nietzsche, who stand under the cultural influence of Christianity while criticizing or even rejecting the claims of Christianity. In this sense, I am a "Christian" reader. "Jewish" will refer simply to those who identify themselves as Jews.

28. Mary Ann Getty, "Paul and the Salvation of Israel: A Perspective on Romans 9–11," CBQ 50 (1988), 456.

29. See the discussion in Gager, *Origins*, 198f.

30. Quotation from personal correspondence with Lloyd Gaston cited in Gager, *Origins*, 198.

31. Stowers, *Rereading*, 327f.

32. In contrast, Gaston defines himself as "a Calvinistic Protestant" and states that "a Christian church with an antisemitic New Testament is abominable, but a Christian church without a New Testament is inconceivable" (*Torah*, 15). Thus, for him, the stakes are specifically religious and theological.

33. Robert Goldenberg in his review of Gager, *Origins*, in *Religious Studies Review* 11(1985), 337 (his emphasis).

34. Michael Wyschogrod, "A Jewish View of Christianity," in *Toward a Theological Encounter. Jewish Understandings of Christianity*, ed. Leon Klenicki (New York, 1991), 119.

35. Wyschogrod, "Jewish View," 119.

36. Gaston, *Torah*, 15.

CHAPTER ONE

Epigraph: Adolph Harnack, *What Is Christianity?* (New York, 1901), 190.

1. For a recent survey of studies on Paul's opposition to the law and Judaism, see Peter Tomson, *Paul and the Jewish Law: Halakha in the Letters of the Apostle to the Gentiles* (Minneapolis and Assen, 1990).

2. See Alan Segal, *Paul the Convert. The Apostolate and Apostasy of Saul the Pharisee* (New Haven, 1990), easily the most thorough and sophisticated treatment of the topic.

3. Stendahl, *Paul Among Jews and Gentiles*, has argued that we should speak of "call" rather than "conversion" in Paul's case (7–23). I have argued elsewhere (Gager, *Origins*, 209–210) that the point, while well taken, does not go to the heart of the matter.

4. The translation here is based on Gaston's version, *Torah*, 78.

5. Compare also his statement in Galatians 1.13 when he speaks of his "former ways (*anastrophē*) in Judaism."

6. The most notable exception is Stowers, *Rereading*, 23–29, where he gives a scathing account of what is implied in the easy use of "Christianity" in Pauline studies.

7. Segal, *Paul the Convert*, 280. Compare a similar statement on the same page: "Paul implies that only those who accept Christ will be saved . . . but, strangely, he does not actually state it." Segal goes on to speak of Paul's deliberately paradoxical language.

8. The term appears in just two New Testament texts (Acts 11.26; 26.28 and 1 Peter 4.16) both of which must be dated well after the year 100 C.E.

9. Pinchas Lapide and Peter Stuhlmacher, *Paul: Rabbi and Apostle* (Minneapolis, 1984), 47.

10. W. D. Davies, "Paul and the People of Israel," *NTS* 24 (1977): 27, makes the point that "Paul was not thinking in terms of what we normally call conversion from one religion to another."

11. See Martin Goodman, *Mission and Conversion : Proselytizing in the Religious History of the Roman Empire* (Oxford, 1994), 70–75.

12. So also Gaston, *Torah*, 6: "It has become more and more clear that it is totally inappropriate to speak of a transition from one religion to another."

13. Alan Segal, *Rebecca's Children. Judaism and Christianity in the Roman World* (Cambridge, 1986),104.

14. In 1 Corinthians 15, where he is defending (again!) his apostolic status, Paul refers to his own vision of the resurrected Christ: "Last of all, as to one untimely born, he appeared also to me. For I am the least of the apostles, unfit to be called an apostle, because I persecuted the church of God" (15.9).

15. See the lengthy discussion in Paula Fredriksen, *From Jesus to Christ. The Origins of the New Testament Images of Jesus* (New Haven, 1988), 142–156; Neil Elliott, *Liberating Paul: The Justice of God and the Politics of the Apostle*, (Sheffield, 1994), 143–149 (relying heavily on Fredriksen); J. C. Beker, *Paul the Apostle. The Triumph of God in Life and Thought* (Philadelphia, 1980), 144; E. P. Sanders, *The Law*, 152; and others.

16. Fredriksen dismisses the view that it was the presence of uncircumcised Gentiles within the Jesus-movement that could have induced Paul's opposition (152f.). Although I find her alternative explanation attractive, that is, that the preaching of the Jesus-movement (crucified messiah, impending end of the world order) might have prompted Jewish fears that Rome would retaliate against the Jews (155), I still consider it possible that a zealous figure like Paul could have been deeply troubled by the idea that Gentiles were being offered redemption outside the law. In any case, multiple factors must have been at work.

17. For a more extensive discussion of the theoretical issues involved, see John G. Gager, "Some Notes on Paul's Conversion," *New Testament Studies* 27 (1981): 697–704.

18. On the supposed tension between Rom. 11.26 ("All Israel will be saved") and 9.27 (quoting Isaiah 10.22–23—"only a remnant will be saved"), see the comments of C. E. B. Cranfield, *A Critical and Exegetical Commentary on the Epistle to the Romans* (Edinburgh, 1979), vol. 2, 501.

19. C. G. Montefiore, a liberal Jewish reader, in *Judaism and St. Paul* (New York, 1915), 138f.

20. James Parkes, a liberal Protestant Christian reader, in *Jesus, Paul and the Jews* (London, 1936), 128.

21. Alfred Loisy, a liberal French Roman Catholic reader, in *L'Épitre aux Galates* (Paris, 1916), 140, 41, 159.

22. William Wrede, a German Protestant reader, in *Paul* (London, 1907), 77.

23. Räisänen, *Law*, 10f. (his emphasis).

24. See Samuel Sandmel, *The Genius of Paul. A Study in History* (New York, 1970), 7: "He was, we may say, a lyric poet like Keats or Shelley; he was no Aquinas or John Dewey."

25. See Hans Conzelmann, *An Outline of the Theology of the New Testament* (New York, 1969), 223–228; compare the discussion in Räisänen, *Law*, 5f.

26. Parkes, *Jesus*, 140: "The abiding influence of his life lies in his mysticism."

27. G. Caird, *The Apostolic Age* (London, 1955), 137: "Some of the difficulties of Paul's thought are paradoxes of the sort that delighted the Semitic mind. Like a true Hebrew Paul was never afraid to hold in tension two ideas which he made no attempt to reconcile." Compare the comment of Wrede (*Paul*, 78): "This fragmentary style of thinking is partly a result of the rabbinical schooling."

28. The position taken by Hans Hübner, *Law in Paul's Thought* (Edinburgh, 1984), 55: "the difference between Galatians and Romans is best explained if we assume that there was a far from trivial theological development on the part of Paul between the two letters."

29. See the discussion in Stendahl, *Paul*, 12–13.

30. See Stowers, *Rereading*, 264.

31. James D. G. Dunn, *The Parting of the Ways Between Christianity and Judaism and their Significance for the Character of Christianity* (London, 1991), 137 (his emphasis). Dunn's view is endorsed by Daniel Boyarin, *A Radical Jew. Paul and the Politics of Identity* (Berkeley, 1994), 136.

32. Dunn, *Parting of the Ways*, 139 (his emphasis). See the critical comments of Stowers, *Rereading*, 27–29.

33. F. C. Baur, *The Church History of the First Three Centuries* (London, 1878),

47; the first German edition appeared in 1853. On Baur's role in the development of New Testament scholarship, see W. G. Kümmel, *The New Testament: The History of the Interpretation of Its Problems* (Nashville, 1972), 127–143.

34. See the critical comments on Käsemann by Nils Dahl, "The One God of Jews and Gentiles," in *Studies in Paul* (Minneapolis, 1977), 191.

35. Dahl in critical comments directed at Käsemann, "The One God of Jews and Gentiles," in *Studies in Paul*, 191.

36. Boyarin, *Radical Jew*, 106.

37. Boyarin, *Radical Jew*, 229 (emphasis added).

38. Rudolph Bultmann, *Primitive Christianity in Its Contemporary Setting* (New York, 1956), 66. On page 65 Bultmann writes that Pharisaic "regulations went to the point of absurdity."

39. Ernst Käsemann, *Commentary on Romans* (Grand Rapids, 1980), 94.

40. Käsemann, *Romans*, 283.

41. E. P. Sanders, *The Law*, 156. On pages 155–157 Sanders offers an extended critique of Käsemann's views of Paul and the law, calling his interpretations "bewildering" and "blatant eisegesis [reading-in], even if eisegesis which rests on long and venerated (perhaps too venerated) tradition." Elsewhere he speaks of his "tortured exegesis" (127).

42. George Foote Moore, "Christian Writers on Judaism," in *Harvard Theological Review* 14(1921): 197–254.

43. E. P. Sanders, *Paul and Palestinian Judaism*, 1–12 and 33–59.

44. Charlotte Klein, *Anti-Judaism in Christian Theology* (Philadelphia, 1978).

45. C. G. Montefiore, *Judaism and St. Paul.*, 21f. Montefiore's point is

that Paul was not a Rabbinic Jew at all and thus not relevant in any way to our understanding of ancient Rabbinic Judaism.

46. Pinchas Lapide in Lapide and Stuhlmacher, *Rabbi*, 39.

47. George Foote Moore, *Judaism in the First Centuries of the Christian Era. The Age of the Tannaim* (Cambridge, 1962), vol. 3, 151. Reflecting on Paul's arguments about the law and sin in Galatians, Moore states that "Paul's argument rests on two premises equally alien to Jewish thought and repugnant to its spirit" (150).

48. Hans Joachim Schoeps, *Paul. The Theology of the Apostle in the Light of Jewish Religious History* (Philadelphia, 1961), 175.

49. Martin Buber, *Two Types of Faith. A Study of the Interpenetration of Judaism and Christianity* (New York, 1961), 55. Buber is referring to Paul's claim in Gal. 5.3 that the whole law must be obeyed.

50. Lapide, *Rabbi*, 37.

51. Leo Baeck, *Judaism and Christianity* (Philadelphia, 1958), 166.

52. Baeck, *Judaism*, 146f. See also, in different ways, Richard Rubinstein, *My Brother Paul* (New York, 1972), 40 ("After Paul became a Christian, he was convinced that the fundamental shortcoming of observance of the Law was its inability to assure men that they would not die"); and Schoeps, *Paul*, 55 (". . . aspects of his consciousness were so changed by his call that the zealot for the law could become its critic"). Leo Baeck, in his essay "The Faith of Paul," insists that Paul's thought is Jewish to the core.

53. See especially among Jewish critics—Schoeps, *Paul*, 260; Montefiore, *Judaism and St. Paul*, 22; Joseph Klausner, *From Jesus to Paul* (New York, 1943), 450–466 (a chapter entitled "Paul, the Hellenistic Jew"); Sandmel, *Genius*, 45; and Boyarin, *Radical Jew*, passim.

54. Moore, *Judaism*, vol. 3, 151.

55. Sandmel, *Genius*, 112. At the same time, Sandmel adds that Paul was "critical of his inherited Judaism" (112).

56. Buber, *Two Types*, 54; "works of the Law" here refers to Gal. 3. 10 ("All who rely on works of the law are under a curse").

57. Segal, *Rebecca's Children*, 111; compare *Paul the Convert*, 276: "In Galatians, Paul has been concerned with clarifying that new converts did not have to observe Torah."

58. See Maurice Wiles in *The Divine Apostle*.

59. J. C. Beker makes the same point in his *Paul the Apostle*, 341: "The rest of the New Testament . . . allows much less fruitful confrontation because it is no longer interested in Judaism as a living alternative. Instead, Judaism has in most of the New Testament become a polemical foil and a historical enemy."

60. Meyer, "Romans 10:4," 72.

61. Stendahl, *Paul*, 86f.

62. See Tomson, *Paul and the Jewish Law*, 245.

63. See the discussion in Francis Watson, *Paul, Judaism and the Gentiles* (Cambridge, 1986), 4–7.

64. Rudolf Bultmann, in "Romans 7 and the Anthropology of Paul," in *Existence and Faith. Shorter Writings* (New York, 1960), 151 (emphasis added).

65. Günther Bornkamm, *Paul* (New York, 1971), 94f.

66. Ernst Käsemann, *New Testament Questions of Today* (London, 1971), 184.

67. "Justification and Salvation History in the Epistle to the Romans," *Perspectives on Paul* (Philadelphia, 1971), 71f. (emphasis added).

68. See Stowers, *Rereading*, 10.

69. Maurice Goguel, *The Birth of Christianity* (London, 1953), 195.

70. See notes 42–44.

71. The term is Elliott's; see *Liberating Paul*, 66–68.

72. Schweitzer, *Paul and His Interpreters* (New York, 1964), 238.

73. For example, Schweitzer, *Paul and His Interpreters*, 241.

74. W. D. Davies, *Paul and Rabbinic Judaism, Some Rabbinic Elements in Pauline Theology* (London, 1958).

75. Tomson, *Jewish Law*, 1.

76. Schoeps, *Paul*, 262.

77. David Flusser, "Die Christenheit nach dem Apostelkonzil," in *Judaism and Christianity* (Jerusalem, 1972), 117.

CHAPTER TWO

Epigraph: Michael Wyschogrod, "The Impact of Dialogue with Christianity on My Self-Understanding as a Jew," in *Die Hebräische Bibel und ihre zweifache Nachgeschichte. Festschrift für Rolf Rendtorff zum 65. Geburtstag*, ed. E. Blum, C. Macholz, and E. Stegemann (Neukirchen, 1990), 731.

1. Schoeps, *Paul*, 175.

2. Moore. *Judaism in the First Centuries*, vol. 3, 151. Reflecting on Paul's arguments about the law and sin in Galatians, Moore states that "Paul's argument rests on two premises equally alien to Jewish thought and repugnant to its spirit" (150).

3. Wyschogrod, "The Impact of Dialogue," 731f. Wyschogrod appears to waver a bit, but in the end seems convinced (733). His statement in "A Jewish View of Christianity," 119, is decisive: "The debate concerned Gentiles. . . . If all this is true, then it puts Paul's criticisms of the law in a totally new light. Paul's letters in which he criticizes the law were written to Gentiles who were being influenced by Jewish Jesus-believers to accept circumcision and Torah observance . . . he has a specific purpose in mind: to dissuade Gentile Jesus-believers from placing themselves under the obligations of the Torah."

4. Gaston, *Torah*, 23 (his emphasis).

5. Delivered at Austin Presbyterian Seminary in 1963 and at Colgate Rochester Divinity School in 1964.

6. Delivered at the American Psychological Association in 1961. Both now printed in Stendahl, *Paul*.

7. "I am convinced that Pauline theology has its organizing center in Paul's apostolic perception of his mission to the Gentiles." Stendahl, *Final Account*, ix.

8. Stendahl, *Paul*, 22.

9. Stendahl focuses on Galatians 3.23f. that speaks of the law as a *paidagô-gos eis christon* ("until Christ comes"). Comparing the King James and the RSV versions, Stendahl concludes that they represent "two radically, drastically, and absolutely opposed understandings of the same Greek phrase" Stendahl, *Paul*, 18.

10. Stendahl, *Final Account*, 6.

11. Stendahl, *Paul*, 18.

12. Stendahl, *Final Account*, 38. "In other words, 'Get off the backs of the Jews, and leave them in the hands of God.' God has the power to realize their salvation, which is definitely not cast in christological terms" (40).

13. Sanders, *Paul and Palestinian Judaism*, 75.

14. Wyschogrod, "Impact," 731. Compare also Frank Thielman, *From Plight to Solution. A Jewish Framework for Understanding Paul's View of the Law in Galatians and Romans* (Leiden, 1989), 1: "Jewish scholarship has always taken exception to this idea, claiming that no Jew believes that the law must be kept in its entirety in order to attain salvation."

15. Sanders, *The Law*, 156.

16. Sanders, *Paul and Palestinian Judaism*, 551.

17. Sanders, *Paul and Palestinian Judaism*, 552.

18. Sanders, 551f.

19. Sanders, *The Law*, 207.

20. See the critical comments by Stowers, *Rereading*, 24–26.

21. Sanders, *The Law*, 208.

22. For example, Sanders, *Paul and Palestinian Judaism*, 451, 463, 490, and so on.

23. Sanders, *Paul and Palestinian Judaism*, 490.

24. *Sanders, Paul and Palestinian Judaism*, 551.

25. James D. G. Dunn, *The Parting of the Ways*, 137 (his emphasis).

26. James D. G. Dunn, "The New Perspective on Paul: Paul and the Law," in *The Romans Debate*, ed. Karl Donfried (Peabody, 1991), 307

27. James D. G. Dunn, *Romans: Word Biblical Commentary* (Dallas, 1988), 51.

28. Dunn, *Romans*, 86.

29. Dunn, *Parting of the Ways*, 139 (his emphasis).

30. See the critical comments of Stowers, *Rereading*, 27–29; for example, "The evidence of Jewish texts betrays the implausibility of Dunn's presumed reader" (29). Dunn's selection of proof-texts ("New Perspective," 303–306) is highly tendentious and runs against the grain of much recent scholarship.

31. In his *The Theology of Paul's Letter to the Galatians* (Cambridge, 1993) Dunn insists that Paul never thought of himself as a convert from Judaism and that it is wrong to speak of Judaism and Christianity as separate religions at that time (40f.). Yet he speaks throughout of Christian Jews and Gentiles.

32. Paul Meyer, "Romans 10:4," 72.

33. Franz Mussner, *Tractate on the Jews* (Philadelphia, 1984), 143.

34. Gaston, *Torah*, 92.

35. Stowers, *Rereading*, 129.

36. Compare Romans 15.15f.: "I have written to you very boldly by way of a reminder, because of the grace given to me by God to be a minister of Christ Jesus to the Gentiles."

37. Acts 14.1; 17.1 etc. Ronald Hock, in his book *The Social Context of Paul's Ministry* (Philadelphia, 1980), contends that Paul also combined his teaching/preaching with his trade as a tent-maker.

38. In 1 Thessalonians 2.16 Paul speaks of Jews in the area as "hindering us from speaking to Gentiles." And in 2 Corinthians 11. 24–26 he reports that he had been in danger from his own people and that "five times I have received at the hands of the Jews the forty lashes less one." I take the lashes to mean that he had been punished, as a Jew, by local synagogue authorities

for his disruptive teaching/preaching to and about Gentiles.

39. Gaston, *Torah*, 4.

40. Gaston, *Torah*, 28.

41. Sanders, *Paul and Palestinian Judaism*, 483.

42. Hans Hübner, *Law in Paul's Thought*, 109f. (his emphasis).

43. Hübner, *Law*, 110.

44. Gaston, *Torah*, 116–134.

45. Sanders, *The Law*, 178.

46. W. D. Davies, *Paul and Rabbinic Judaism*, 324.

47. Sanders, *The Law*, 152.

48. Gaston, *Torah*, 28.

49. Stefan Meissner, *Die Heimholung des Ketzers. Studien zur jüdischen Auseinandersetzung mit Paulus* (Tübingen, 1996), 6.

50. Klausner, *From Jesus to Paul*, 453.

51. Klausner, *From Jesus to Paul*, 453f.

52. Schoeps, *Paul*, 259.

53. Boyarin, *A Radical Jew*, 257.

54. Boyarin, *A Radical Jew*, 92.

55. Rubinstein, *My Brother Paul*, 114: "the issues to which Paul addressed

himself arose entirely within the religious and symbolic universe of Judaism of his time and [that] he never ceased to regard himself as a believing, faithful Jew."

56. Gaston, *Torah*, 25–29; see esp. the additional texts cited on 197, n. 53.

57. Gaston, *Torah*, 30.

58. Dunn, "New Perspective," 301f.

59. Stowers, *Rereading*, 327.

60. Meyer, "Romans 10:4," 66.

61. Tomson, *Jewish Law*, 237.

62. Lapide and Stuhlmacher, *Rabbi*, 42.

63. Wyschogrod, "Impact," 733.

64. David Flusser, *Das Christentum—eine jüdische Religion* (Munich, 1990), 135.

65. See Gerd Luedemann, *Opposition to Paul in Jewish Christianity*.

66. Gaston, *Torah*, 77.

67. W. D. Davies, "People of Israel," 27.

68. J. C. Beker, *Paul the Apostle*, 334f.

69. Mussner, *Tractate*, 34.

70. Gaston, *Torah*, 148.

71. Klausner, *Jesus to Paul*, 453 (his emphasis).

72. Segal, *Paul the Convert*, 280.

73. Stowers, *Rereading*, 205f.

74. Stowers, *Rereading*, 205.

75. Stowers, *Rereading*, 132.

76. Gaston, *Torah*, 33.

77. To confirm his claim Paul cites four biblical passages—Ps. 18.49; Deut. 32.43; Ps. 117.1; and Isa. 11.10—each of which speaks of God's redemption of the Gentiles.

78. Stowers, *Rereading*, 308.

79. Baeck, "Faith of Paul," 108.

80. See the discussion in Terence Donaldson, *Paul and the Gentiles. Remapping the Apostle's Convictional World* (Minneapolis, 1997), 51–78.

81. Donaldson, 74.

82. See the discussion in Joyce Reynolds and Robert Tannenbaum, *Jews and God-Fearers at Aphrodisias* (Cambridge, 1987), 41f.

83. Philo, *Questions and Answers on Exodus*, 2.2.

84. Josephus, *Jewish Antiquities*, 20.41.

85. Stowers, *Rereading*, 155. As examples, Stowers cites Lev. 26.41; Deut. 10.16; 30.6; Jer. 4.4; 9.25f.; Ezech. 44.7–9, all of which speak of circumcision of the heart.

86. G. Eichholz, *Die Theologie des Paulus im Umriss* (Neukirchen, 1972), 296.

87. Stowers, *Rereading*, 296; compare Gaston, *Torah*, 140f.

88. Josephus, *Against Apion*, 2.282f.

89. Josephus, *Against Apion*, 2.210.

90. So Josephus, *Antiquities* 4.238; and the Mishnah, *Makkot* 3.10f. Josephus, the Mishnah, and Paul use the technical phrase "forty lashes minus one" to describe the punishment.

91. Gaston, *Torah*, 233, n. 39 among others, holds this passage to be a later scribal interpolation.

92. Despite recent attempts to hold that the author of Acts did not subscribe to the rejection-replacement view of Israel, I remain convinced that this is precisely the author's view . Those Jews who do accept the gospel preached by the apostles cease to be Jews; Israel as a people is disobedient. For the alternative view, see J. B. Tyson, *Luke—Acts and the Jewish People* (Minneapolis, 1988), esp. the essay by D. Tiede.

93. Tertullian, *Against Marcion*, 5.2.1.

94. Dahl, *Studies*, 142.

95. Richard Hays, *Echoes of Scripture in the Letters of Paul* (New Haven, 1989), 60.

96. William Campbell, "Romans III as a Key to the Structure and Thought of the Letter, " in Donfried, *The Romans Debate*, 261.

97. Rudolf Bultmann, *Der Stil der paulinischen Predigt und die kynisch-stoische Diatribe* (Göttingen, 1984; first published in 1910).

98. Arnaldo Momigliano, *The Development of Greek Biography* (Cambridge, 1971). Speaking of the influence of Plato's *Letter 7*, Momigliano comments that "one vaguely feels the Platonic precedent in Epicurus, Seneca and per-

haps St. Paul" (62).

99. George Kennedy, *New Testament Interpretation through Rhetorical Criticism* (Chapel Hill, 1984) 9f., 144–156.

100. Stowers, *Rereading*, and his earlier work, *The Diatribe and Paul's Letter to the Romans*.

101. Elliott, *Liberating Paul*, 85f. and *The Rhetoric of Romans. Argumentative Constraint and Strategy and Paul's Dialogue with Judaism* (Sheffield, 1990), esp. 60–67.

102. Lodge, *Analysis*.

103. Stowers, *Rereading*, 16.

104. See the extended discussion in Stowers, *Rereading*, 16–21.

105. W. G. Kümmel, *Römer 7 und die Bekehrung des Paulus* (Leipzig, 1929).

106. See the extended discussion in Stowers, *Rereading*, 264–284.

107. Nilus, *Epistles*, vol. 1, nos.152f. (*PG*, vol. 79, columns 145f.).

108. Rudolf Bultmann, *Theology of the New Testament* (New York, 1951), vol. 1, 242.

109. Käsemann, *Romans*, 68.

110. Epictetus, *Diatribes* 2.19.19.

111. Epictetus, *Diatribes* 2.9.19.

112. Lodge, *Analysis*, 28, 165, 191.

113. Wayne Booth, *The Rhetoric of Fiction* (Chicago, 1983), 295.

114. Gaston, *Torah*, 8.

115. Stowers, *Rereading*, 326.

116. Davies, "People of Israel," 22.

117. See Ernst Käsemann, "Justification and Salvation History," *Perspectives on Paul*, 64; the essay is a response to Stendahl's "The Apostle Paul and the Introspective Conscience of the West."

CHAPTER THREE

Epigraph: Franz Mussner, *Traktat über die Juden* (Munich, 1979), 144.

1. H. D. Betz, *A Commentary on Paul's Letter to the Galatians* (Philadelphia, 1979), 7, argues that the gospel of Paul's opponents "must have been the same as Paul's" in other respects. This seems most unlikely. To the degree that they were associated with the Jerusalem church, I would agree with Gaston. "The theology of Paul and the theology of Jerusalem are completely different," *Torah*, 115, see his essay "Paul and Jerusalem."

2. Gaston, *Torah*, 4.

3. Betz, *Galatians*, 14–24.

4. Momigliano, *Greek Biography*, 62.

5. Betz, *Galatians*, 25. It should be noted here that rhetoric and "magic" are more closely related than might be imagined, for both seek to accomplish their goals through the manipulation of language. Furthermore, they are often portrayed as similar in Greek literature.

6. Kennedy, *New Testament Interpretation*, 144–152. See also Sam K. Williams, *Galatians* (Nashville, 1997), 29–31.

7. See Philippians 3.1–11 and 2 Corinthians 11.21–12.13.

8. Betz, *Galatians*, 116.

9. Sanders, *The Law*, 19.

10. Sanders, *The Law*, 19f.

11. Sanders, *The Law*, 30.

12. James D. G. Dunn, "The New Perspective on Paul," *Bulletin of John Rylands Library* 65 (1983): 106.

13. Dunn, "New Perspective," 110.

14. Dunn, "New Perspective," 120.

15. There is precedent in Judaism for this position. The Sifra, a Rabbinic commentary to Leviticus (fourth century?), quotes Rabbi Jeremiah/Yirmiya as offering the following interpretation of Lev. 18.5 ("You should keep my laws and my statutes, by doing which a man shall live"): R. Yirmiya was wont to say, "Whence do you say that even a gentile who does the Torah, behold he is like the high priest?" The passage appears to suggest that Gentiles do not convert but rather "do the Torah." The phrase "who does the Torah" (*oseh torah*) is significant here for two reasons: first, it is close to the Pauline expression "works of the law/Torah"; and second, because it is used specifically of Gentiles. I rely here on an unpublished paper of Marc Hirshman, "Rabbinic Universalism in the Second and Third Centuries." For a discussion of the phrase "works of the Torah" (*ma'asei ha-torah*) in 4QMMT, an important text from Qumran, see John Kampen, "4QMMT and New Testament Studies," in *Reading 4QMMT: New Perspectives on Qumran Law and History*, eds. John Kampen and Moshe J. Bernstein (Atlanta, 1996), 138–143.

16. See the full discussion in Gaston, *Torah*, 76–79.

17. Mussner, *Tractate*, 144 (emphasis added).

18. Sanders, *The Law*, 19.

19. Norman H. Young, "Who's Cursed—And Why? (Galatians 3:10–14)," *Journal of Biblical Literature* 117 (1998): 90f. contends that Paul's "concern is not the deliverance of the Gentiles from their past condemnation but rather the freeing of them in the present." I heartily agree with the second claim but cannot escape the sense that Paul sees their present threat as a return to their former condition.

20. Here Martyn, *Galatians*, misses the point altogether; see 327 ("the curse of the Law was universal, falling on every human being . . . Jew and Gentile"); cf. also 317.

21. See Gaston, *Torah*, 74: "The enclosing verses speak explicitly of Gentiles, and one would expect that the enclosed verses, which speak of the law as a curse, would also speak . . . of Gentiles."

22. Gaston, *Torah*, 79.

23. Sanders, *The Law*, 31, summarizing the arguments in Chapter 3, although Sanders goes on to state that Paul is concerned with the status of Gentiles and Jews.

24. See the full discussion in Gaston, *Torah*, 35–44 ("Angels and Gentiles in Early Judaism and Paul").

25. See Marcel Simon, *Verus Israel. A Study of the Relations between Christians and Jews in the Roman Empire (135–425)* (London, 1996), 88f. on the notion of *deuterosis*, according to which God imposed the rigorous ritual commandments on the Jews as punishment for their idolatry at Sinai.

26. Betz, *Galatians*, 165, 170.

27. See the useful discussion in Betz, *Galatians*, 177.

28. Betz, *Galatians*, 178.

29. Gaston, *Torah*, 33f.

30. Martyn, *Galatians*, 40f. Compare 382: "It is Christ and the community of those incorporated into him who lie beyond religious distinctions [i.e., Jew and Gentile]."

31. Gaston, *Torah*, 29.

32. Sanders, *The Law*, 69, is typical here: "Jews were under the law, while pagans were under 'beings' which are not actually gods."

33. On Paul's use of the term see Hays, *Echoes*, 116.

34. See Rosemary Ruether, *Faith and Fratricide* (New York, 1974), 102f., 134f.

35. A Jewish text from this period, the book of Jubilees, makes just this point in 16.17–18.

36. Hays, *Echoes*, 112.

37. Hays, *Echoes*, 112.

38. Hays, *Echoes*, 114.

39. Hays, *Echoes*, 111.

40. Hays, *Echoes*, 117.

41. Hays, *Echoes*, 116.

42. Gaston, *Torah*, 91, translates the whole of v. 25 as follows, eliminating the inexplicably negative reference to the earthly Jerusalem found in most common translations (e.g., RSV—"She [Hagar] corresponds to the present Jerusalem, for she is in slavery with her children"): "It [Sinai] is in the opposite column [*sustoichei*] from the present Jerusalem." The logic runs as follows:

"the slavery Sinai covenant is Hagar, for Sinai is in Arabia; that is the opposite of Jerusalem, for Hagar is in slavery; Jerusalem is free and our mother, for Isaiah 54 says so."

43. Gaston, *Torah*, 86. Gaston cites a later Rabbinic text, a midrash on Deuteronomy, *Mekilta*, Bahodesh 5, that makes a similar point.

44. Gaston, *Torah*, 87.

45. See Williams, *Galatians*, 131.

46. See also Martyn, *Galatians*, 447–457. Martyn views the entire Hagar–Sarah discussion as directed against Paul's opponents and interprets the two covenants as two antithetical conceptions of the mission to the Gentiles: Hagar = slavery = newly circumcised Gentiles (the opponents); Sarah = freedom = Gentiles in Christ (Paul).

47. Hays, *Echoes*, 115f.

48. Hays, *Echoes*, 114.

49. Tomson, *Jewish Law*, 88f. The formula appears in the Jerusalem Talmud (*Demai* 2.5); in Sifra, *Qedoshim* 8.3; in the Babylonian Talmud (*Bekhoroth* 30b); and other places.

50. Sanders, *Law*, 28.

51. Sanders, *Law*, 27.

52. See Gaston, *Torah*, 28.

53. See Williams, *Galatians*, 142.

CHAPTER FOUR

Epigraph: Gaston, *Torah*, 134.

1. See the discussion in Martyn, *Galatians*, 30–34.

2. Martyn, *Galatians*, 31.

3. Dahl, *Studies in Paul*, 142.

4. Hays, *Echoes*, 60.

5. W. G. Kümmel, *Introduction to the New Testament*, 17th edition (Nashville, 1975), 309–310.

6. See the extensive discussion of Neil Elliott, *The Rhetoric of Romans*, 9–43; and on Romans as a debate with Judaism, 167–223.

7. Stowers, *Rereading*, puts it this way: "The erasure [of the Gentile audience] is a hermeneutical move that facilitates reading the letter as canonical scripture of the orthodox catholic church" (33).

8. Stowers, *Rereading*, 36.

9. Stowers, *Rereading*, 40.

10. Getty, "Salvation of Israel," 457.

11. This translation follows that of Stowers, *Rereading*, 199.

12. Sanders, *The Law*, 30.

13. Sanders, *The Law*, 30

14. C.E.B. Cranfield, *The Epistle to the Romans* (Edinburgh, 1975), vol. 1, 227. See the extended discussion in Elliott, *Rhetoric*, 216–219.

15. Gaston, *Torah*, 118, give a somewhat different reading of this phrase, translating it as "for the Jew of course, but also for the Greeks."

16. The translation given here "faith of Christ" renders the Greek *pistis christou*. Gaston and others have argued that the Greek phrase, normally translated as "faith in Christ," sometimes implies not faith in Christ but rather Christ's faithfulness or loyalty, like Abraham's. My view is that this rendering is correct in many instances, even if not in every one. In any case, the sometimes hot debate over the proper translation of the phrase is not central to the overall argument presented here.

17. Stowers, *Rereading*, 307.

18. Stowers, *Rereading*, 306. See also K. Stendahl, *Final Account*, ix: "I am convinced that Pauline theology has its organizing center in Paul's perception of his mission to the Gentiles. Consequently, Romans is central to our understanding of Paul, not because of its doctrine of justification [= *dikaiosunê*], but because the doctrine of justification is here in its original and authentic setting: as an argument for the status of Paul's Gentile converts on the model of Abraham (Romans 4)."

19. Gaston's observation here is useful: "Divine impartiality, [which] must not be confused with evenhandedness. The phrase "there is no partiality with God" is used Biblically (for example, Deut. 10.17 and 18) to show that there precisely is partiality, namely, toward the disadvantaged," *Torah*, 120.

20. See Stowers, *Rereading*, 122: "Rom 1:18–32 contains compressed allusions to Jewish versions of decline narratives." See also Elliott, *Rhetoric*, 173ff., who draws attention to similar indictments of Gentile sinning in the Wisdom of Solomon 13–14 and Philo.

21. Käsemann, *Romans*, 53f.

22. Elliott, *Rhetoric*, 180, uses the phrase to summarize the views of many traditional readers. In general, Elliott offers a devastating criticism of the traditional view. On page 187, Elliott criticizes, correctly, my earlier reading of

the text (Gager, *Origins*, 214–17, 248f.).

23. Elliott, *Rhetoric*, 180f. Elliott points to a series of Jewish texts, Rabbinic and others, in which smugness regarding guaranteed forgiveness is rejected.

24. Gaston, *Torah*, 120.

25. See the full discussion of Jouette Bassler, *Divine Impartiality: Paul and a Theological Axiom* (Chico, 1982), 129–34.

26. Stowers, *Rereading*, 141.

27. Sanders, *The Law*, 126.

28. Sanders, *The Law*, 127.

29. Sanders, *The Law*, 129 (emphasis added).

30. O'Neill, *Romans*, 52.

31. See also Gaston, *Torah*, 138, who observes that Sanders and O'Neill offer sensible readings of the text, that is, that Paul is here urging Jews (not Gentiles) to keep the law better, but laments that they seem unable to understand why Paul "would want to say that."

32. See Sanders, *The Law*, 131.

33. Elliott, *Rhetoric*, 186f., comments that the statement in 2.12b–13, that is, that Jews are judged on whether they do what the law requires, is "indistinguishable from what E. P. Sanders has called 'covenantal nomism'."

34. Again, Elliott's paraphrase (187) of traditional interpretations.

35. Stowers, *Rereading*, 142.

36. Käsemann, *Romans*, 68.

37. Cranfield, *Romans*, vol. 1, 168. For a more complete listing of similar views, see Stowers, *Rereading*, 143f. and Elliott, *Rhetoric*, 191–98.

38. See Gaston, *Torah*, 139: "Paul is accusing not all Jews but Jewish missionaries, and he is accusing not all missionaries but only some (cf. 3:3). . . . But most important he does so not to speak of Jewish 'theology' but of the bad effect such activity has for attracting proselytes." See also Origen, in his commentary on Romans, who insists that Paul is addressing not the Jews but only the false Jew, one in name only; see Peter Gorday, *Principles of Patristic Exegesis. Romans 9–11 in Origen, John Chrysostom, and Augustine* (New York, 1983), 56f.

39. See the earlier discussion, 107.

40. Stowers, *Rereading*, 153.

41. See Elliott, *Rhetoric*, 197f.

42. Käsemann, *Romans*, 72 and 73.

43. Stowers, *Rereading*, 155.

44. See again Käsemann, 72; see the discussion in Elliott, *Rhetoric*, 199.

45. Philo, *On Rewards and Punishments* 152 (translation from F. H. Colson, *Philo* [Cambridge, 1960], vol. 8, 409.)

46. Stowers, *Rereading*, 158.

47. Stowers has proposed a novel approach to the language of 3.1–9. He reads it as a dialogue between Paul and the Jewish teacher, based on the model of similar dialogues in Epictetus and Dio Chrysostom. Paul speaks in verses 2–3, 5, 7–8, 9b; the teacher in verses 1, 4, 6, and 9a.

48. See the extensive discussion in Stowers, *Rereading*, 167–175. He points in particular to Ezekiel 36.23–26 and Isaiah 52.5.

49. Williams, "The 'Righteousness of God' in Romans," *JBL* 99 (1980): 241–90.

50. Stowers, *Rereading*, 171.

51. Stowers, *Rereading*, 171.

52. Gaston argues that the language of 3.1–9 points not to Jewish but to Gentile objections (*Torah*, 121). This is a possible reading. But in any case it does not change the larger picture.

53. Stowers, *Rereading*, 181.

54. Stowers, *Rereading*, 172.

55. Gaston, *Torah*, 121,

56. Elliott, *Rhetoric*, 208.

57. See also, among others, Sanders, Beker, and Elliott.

58. Stowers, *Rereading*, 185.

59. George Howard, "Romans 3:21–31 and the Inclusion of the Gentiles," *Harvard Theological Review* 63 (1970): 230.

60. Gaston, *Torah*, 122.

61. George Howard, *Paul: Crisis in Galatia* (Cambridge, 1990; second edition), xxviii–xxix.

62. See Howard, "Romans 3:21–31," p. 231 and Sam Williams, *Jesus' Death as Saving Event: The Background and Origin of a Concept* (Missoula, 1975), 19–34.

63. Käsemann, *Romans*, 102.

64. See the extensive discussion in Stowers, *Rereading*, 231–37.

65. This reading of boasting in 3.27 and elsewhere in Romans represents a modification of my earlier view as expressed in Gager, *Origins*, 248f. I am also sensitive to Elliott's observation (*Rhetoric*, 214) that "[t]he reasons for considering *kauchēsis* in 3.27 to mean specifically and exclusively Jewish boasting are similarly inadequate." I also find that my use of terms like "exclusive access" and "collective exclusivity" are no longer appropriate.

66. On this translation of 4.1, which departs significantly from the RSV, see Gaston, *Torah*, 124f. and Stowers, *Rereading*, 241f.

67. See the discussions in Gaston, *Torah*, 51–56.

68. Cranfield, *Romans*, vol. 1, 227. See the discussion in Elliott, *Rhetoric*, 216–221.

69. Gaston, *Torah*, 62.

70. See Young, "Who's Cursed," 81.

71. Howard, "Romans 3:21–31," 231.

72. Howard, *Paul*, xxviii-xxix.

73. Stowers, *Rereading*, 251.

74. Stendahl, *Paul*, 86f. and 92–94.

75. Stowers, *Rereading*, 264–84.

76. *Medea*, lines 1077–1080. See the lengthy discussion in Stowers, *Rereading*, 260–64.

77. Stowers, *Rereading*, 280.

78. So Stowers, *Rereading*, 264–269.

79. Nilus, *Epistles*, vol. 1, no. 152 (*PG*, vol. 79, columns 145f.).

80. Nilus, *Epistles*, no. 153.

81. Stowers, *Rereading*, 278.

82. F. W. Beare, *St. Paul and His Letters* (London, 1962), 103f.

83. Räisänen, *Paul and the Law*, 264.

84. Stendahl, *Paul*, 4.

85. Cranfield, *Romans*, vol. 2, 445. See also the important discussions of Nils Dahl, *Studies*, 139–42.; Elliott, *Rhetoric*, 253–75; and Stowers, *Rereading*, 285–87.

86. Räisänen, *Paul and the Law*, 264.

87. Quintilian, *Institutes*, 6.2.34.

88. See Elliott, *Rhetoric*, 262.

89. Stowers, *Rereading*, 293.

90. Gaston, *Torah*, 147.

91. Gaston, *Torah*, 94

92. Stowers, *Rereading*, 301f.

93. Dahl, *Paul*, 146.

94. Cranfield, *Romans*, 512.

95. See the discussion in Gaston, *Torah*, 129.

96. Meyer, "Romans 10:4," 64.

97. Gaston, *Torah*, 92.

98. Stowers, *Rereading*, 299.

99. Lodge, *Analysis*, 132, 166.

100. Meyer, "Romans 10:4," 72.

101. See the discussion in Cranfield, *Romans*, 517–519. His list of names includes Lietzmann, Lagrange, Dodd, Gaugler, Michel, Käsemann, Leenhardt, Barrett, and Schlier.

102. Meyer, "Romans 10:4," 72.

103. Stowers, *Rereading*, 308.

104. Stowers, *Rereading*, 307.

105. Gaston, *Torah*, 142.

106. Lodge, *Analysis*, 165.

107. Lodge, *Analysis*, 133 (his emphasis).

108. Gaston, *Torah*, 142.

109. P. E. Dinter, "The Remnant of Israel and the Stone of Stumbling in Zion according to Paul (Romans 9–11)" (Ph.D. dissertation, Union Theological Seminary, New York, 1980).

110. Dinter, "The Remnant of Israel," 87, 168.

111. Räisänen, "Paul, God, and Israel: Romans 9-11 in Recent Research," in *The Social World of Formative Christianity and Judaism: Essays in Tribute to Howard Clark Kee*, ed. J. Neusner (Philadelphia, 1988), 187.

112. Stowers, *Rereading*, 312–16.

113. Stendahl, *Final Account*, 6.

114. Gaston, *Torah*, 140. He cites G. Eichholz, *Die Theologie des Paulus* 296, to the effect that Chapter 9–11 are to be taken "nicht primär als israelkritisch— sondern als kirchenkritisch" ("not primarily as critical of Judaism—but as critical of the church").

115. The title of his Chapter 10 is "A Warning . . . to Gentiles."

116. Stendahl, *Paul*, 4.

117. Stendahl, *Paul*. See also Robin Scroggs, "Paul as Rhetorician: Two Homilies in Romans 1–11," in *Jews, Greeks and Christians*, ed. R. Hamerton-Kelly and Scroggs (Leiden, 1976), 276: "It is God who is emphasized in these chapters . . . while the figure of Christ remains in the background."

118. Davies, "People of Israel," 25. Davies lays out as possible the view that for Paul "the future does not bring Israel into connection with the Christ of the new covenant for Gentiles at all" (26). In the end, however, he opts for the traditional view, that is, that Israel will and must come to Jesus Christ.

119. Getty, "Perspective," 461.

120. Getty, "Perspective." See also Gaston, *Torah*, 143f., esp. n. 45.

121. Davies, "People of Israel," 26.

122. Lodge, *Analysis*, 199.

123. Gaston, *Torah*, 33.

124. Stowers, *Rereading*, 306.

NOTES TO CHAPTER FIVE

Epigraph: An early Christian text quoting an unnamed "heretic" (4.6).

1. See Gager, *Origins*, 198f.

2. Elliott, *Rhetoric*, 296f.

3. Stowers, *Rereading*, 205.

4. Gaston, *Torah*, 78f.

5. J. Louis Martyn, *Galatians*, 464.

6. See note 6, page 154 of this volume.

7. See the comments of Mitchell, "Chrysostom," 94f.

8. See Birger A. Pearson, "1 Thessalonians 2:13–16: A Deutero-Pauline Interpolation," *Harvard Theological Review* 64 (1971): 79–94.

9. Stowers, *Rereading*, 178.

10. Bloom, *Poetics of Influence* (New Haven, 1988), 396.

11. Bloom, *Poetics*.

12. Justin Taylor and Etienne Nodet, *The Origins of Christianity. An Exploration* (Collegeville, Minn., 1998), 321.

13. Taylor and Nodet, *Origins*, 346.

14. Gaston, *Torah*, 2.

INDEX OF SUBJECTS

INDEX OF MODERN SCHOLARS

INDEX OF ANCIENT TEXTS